Management for Professionals

More information about this series at http://www.springer.com/series/10101

Yacob Khojasteh

Production Control Systems

A Guide to Enhance Performance of Pull Systems

Springer

Yacob Khojasteh
Graduate School of Global Studies
Sophia University
Tokyo, Japan

ISSN 2192-8096 ISSN 2192-810X (electronic)
Management for Professionals
ISBN 978-4-431-55196-6 ISBN 978-4-431-55197-3 (eBook)
DOI 10.1007/978-4-431-55197-3

Library of Congress Control Number: 2015940094

Springer Tokyo Heidelberg New York Dordrecht London
© Springer Japan 2016

This work is subject to copyright. All rights are reserved by the Publisher, whether the whole or part of the material is concerned, specifically the rights of translation, reprinting, reuse of illustrations, recitation, broadcasting, reproduction on microfilms or in any other physical way, and transmission or information storage and retrieval, electronic adaptation, computer software, or by similar or dissimilar methodology now known or hereafter developed.

The use of general descriptive names, registered names, trademarks, service marks, etc. in this publication does not imply, even in the absence of a specific statement, that such names are exempt from the relevant protective laws and regulations and therefore free for general use.

The publisher, the authors and the editors are safe to assume that the advice and information in this book are believed to be true and accurate at the date of publication. Neither the publisher nor the authors or the editors give a warranty, express or implied, with respect to the material contained herein or for any errors or omissions that may have been made.

Printed on acid-free paper

Springer Japan KK is part of Springer Science+Business Media (www.springer.com)

Foreword

Production control systems represent an area of vital importance for the efficiency of operations management in companies, as they heavily impact on lead times, work-in-process, and machine utilization. In some cases, using the most suitable production control system constitutes a competitive advantage. Their study and analysis can be traced back to the beginning of the past century and now constitutes a mature field of knowledge.

In this context, a book like this one is highly welcome. In their pages, the author aims to establish a unified view of production control policies and to set up a framework for production control policies. The focus is put on traditional pull production control systems, which are extensively used in practice. The analysis of assembly production process carried out in the book is of particular interest, as this type of configuration has not been usually dealt with in the literature, at least as much as the more usual serial configuration.

Simulation is used extensively as a mean to tackle the rather complex settings that are discussed in this book and that could not possibly be addressed using different techniques. This has the advantage to keep the prerequisites on an affordable level.

Despite the knowledge on production control systems accumulated since the last century, there are many aspects in these systems that are not yet well understood, together with the unfulfilled promise of generalized, hybrid systems that could eventually inherit the advantages of the classical systems without having too much of their disadvantages. I sincerely hope that this book helps to bring in new developments in this exciting field.

Seville, Spain
March 2015

Jose M. Framinan

Preface

Production control systems (PCS) play a critical role in cost optimization of today's global supply chains. PCS manage the physical material flow on manufacturing plant and are therefore a key driver for inventory levels and production costs. However, selecting a suitable pull production control system is a challenging task for managers because the superiority of one control over the other is controversial.

This book analyzes pull production systems and provides a guideline for managers and practitioners in order to choose and implement a proper control policy in production processes. By employing a proper control policy, the maximum possible throughput of the production system can be achieved with the minimum work-in-process inventory. Kanban, CONWIP, and base-stock as well-known pull control policies are analyzed and analytical comparisons among them in multistage serial and assembly production processes are presented.

Illustrated by carefully chosen examples and supported by analytical solutions, discussions provided in the book clarify the complexity of the comparisons that show there is no general superiority among the control systems. The book explains which structural parameters decide the superiority of one control scheme to the others and how they are related.

I would like to express my gratitude to Prof. Yasutaka Kainuma of Tokyo Metropolitan University, and Prof. Ryo Sato of Yokohama National University for their support and for being inspirational mentors.

I would also like to thank my wife Miya and sons Nima and Yuma for allowing me to devote the time necessary to complete this book. I dedicate this book to them.

Tokyo, Japan
March 2015

Yacob Khojasteh

Contents

1 Introduction 1
    1.1 Toyota Production Systems 2
    1.2 Just-In-Time Systems 3
        1.2.1 JIT Goals 3
    1.3 Objectives 4
    1.4 Structure of the Book 5
    References 6

2 Production Systems 7
    2.1 Pull vs. Push Systems 7
        2.1.1 The Key Differences Between Push and Pull 7
    2.2 Push Systems 8
        2.2.1 MRP 9
            2.2.1.1 MRP Process 11
            2.2.1.2 Lot-Sizing Techniques 13
    2.3 Pull Systems 15
    2.4 Kanban Control Systems 15
        2.4.1 Types of Kanbans and Kanban Rules 16
        2.4.2 The General Method to Determine the Number
            of Kanbans 17
    2.5 Other Pull Control Systems 17
        2.5.1 Base-Stock Control System 17
        2.5.2 CONWIP Control System 18
        2.5.3 Hybrid Control Systems 18
    2.6 The Benefits of Pull Systems 19
    2.7 A Review on Pull Systems 19
    References 22

3 Unified View of Pull Production Systems 25
    3.1 Modeling Convention 25
        3.1.1 Activity Interaction Diagrams 25
    3.2 Pull Systems and Kanban 26
    3.3 Other Pull Systems 27
        3.3.1 CONWIP 27

		3.3.2	Base-Stock	28
		3.3.3	Hybrid Kanban-CONWIP	29
	References			30
4	**A Framework for Production Control Systems**			**31**
	4.1	Token Transactions Systems		31
		4.1.1	Dynamics of a Token Transaction System	32
		4.1.2	Dynamic Properties of a Token Transaction System	33
	4.2	Performance Measures		35
	4.3	Application of the Framework in Comparing Control Systems		35
	References			35
5	**Analysis of Control Systems in Serial Production Lines**			**37**
	5.1	Comparison of Kanban and CONWIP		37
		5.1.1	Analytical Comparison	41
	5.2	Comparison of Base-Stock with Kanban and CONWIP		44
		5.2.1	Comparison of Base-Stock and Kanban	45
		5.2.2	Comparison of Base-stock and CONWIP	51
		5.2.3	Discussions	55
	5.3	Highlights of the Comparison Method		60
	5.4	Conclusions		60
	References			61
6	**Analysis of Control Systems in Assembly Production Processes**			**63**
	6.1	Analysis of Kanban and CONWIP		63
		6.1.1	A Simple Assembly Production Process	63
			6.1.1.1 Numerical Examples	63
			6.1.1.2 Analytical Comparison	70
		6.1.2	Generalized Assembly Production Processes	75
			6.1.2.1 Analytical Comparisons	76
			6.1.2.2 Discussions	80
	6.2	Comparison of Kanban and Base-stock		85
		6.2.1	Analytical Comparison	85
		6.2.2	Example	89
	6.3	Discussion		91
	6.4	Conclusions		94
	References			98
7	**Conclusions and Future Research**			**99**
	7.1	Serial Production Lines		99
	7.2	Assembly Production Processes		100
		7.2.1	Complexity of the Comparisons	100
	7.3	Limitations and Future Study Directions		100
Appendix				**103**
	List of References			103

About the Author

Dr. Yacob Khojasteh is an associate professor at the Graduate School of Global Studies, Sophia University, Tokyo, Japan. He received his Ph.D. in engineering from the University of Tsukuba, Japan. He also received his M.Sc. in policy and planning sciences and in industrial engineering from the University of Tsukuba and Tarbiat Modares University, respectively. He has several years of professional experience in industry and consulting. His research interests include production and operations management, supply chain management, logistics and warehousing, systems modeling and optimization, and lean production systems.

Abbreviations

AID	Activity interaction diagram
APP	Aggregate production planning
BOM	Bill of material
CONWIP	Constant work-in-process
EKCS	Extended Kanban control system
EOQ	Economic order quantity
EPP	Economic part period
FCFC	First-come, first-serve
GKCS	Generalized Kanban control system
JIT	Just-in-time
L4L	Lot-for-lot
LMT	Late material transfer
MPS	Master production schedule
MRP	Material requirements planning
MTO	Make-to-order
PCS	Production control systems
POQ	periodic order quantity
PPB	Part period balancing
SOP	Sales and operations planning
TPS	Toyota production system
VSM	Value stream mapping
WIP	Work-in-process

List of Figures

Fig. 1.1	Structure of the book	5
Fig. 2.1	Material requirements planning	10
Fig. 2.2	A bill of material	11
Fig. 3.1	A serial production line controlled by Kanban	26
Fig. 3.2	A serial production line controlled by CONWIP	28
Fig. 3.3	A serial production line controlled by Base-stock	29
Fig. 3.4	A serial production line controlled by CONWIP-Kanban hybrid	30
Fig. 4.1	A serial production line with four workstations controlled by CONWIP	32
Fig. 5.1	A serial production line with four workstations controlled by Kanban	38
Fig. 5.2	A serial production line with n workstations controlled by CONWIP	41
Fig. 5.3	A serial production line with n workstations controlled by Kanban	41
Fig. 5.4	A serial production line controlled by Base-stock	45
Fig. 5.5	A serial production line with n workstations controlled by Base-stock	46
Fig. 6.1	A simple assembly production process	64
Fig. 6.2	The assembly production process in Fig. 6.1 controlled by CONWIP	64
Fig. 6.3	The assembly production process in Fig. 6.1 controlled by Kanban	65
Fig. 6.4	A general assembly production process with three stages	75
Fig. 6.5	The assembly production process in Fig. 6.1 controlled by Base-stock	86

List of Tables

Table 2.1	Master production schedule based on an aggregate plan	10
Table 2.2	Lead times and on-hand inventories	12
Table 2.3	A gross requirements plan	12
Table 2.4	Net requirements plan for Product A	14
Table 4.1	State transition table of the CONWIP	33
Table 4.2	Cycle means calculation	35
Table 5.1	State transition of case 5.1_KAN for a period	39
Table 5.2	Cycle means of the remaining circuits	40
Table 5.3	State transition of 5.2_BAS for a period	49
Table 5.4	State transition of 5.2_KAN for a period	50
Table 5.5	State transition of 5.3_BAS for a period	54
Table 5.6	State transition of 5.3_CON for a period	55
Table 5.7	State transition of 5.4_BAS for a period	56
Table 5.8	State transition of 5.4_CON for a period	57
Table 5.9	State transition of 5.4_KAN for a period	58
Table 5.10	Parameters in Examples 5.2, 5.3, and 5.4	59
Table 6.1	State transition of the case Assembly-CONWIP-1 for a period	66
Table 6.2	State transition of the case Assembly-CONWIP-2 for a period	68
Table 6.3	State transition of the case Assembly-CONWIP-3 for a period	69
Table 6.4	State transition of the case Assembly-Kanban for a period	71
Table 6.5	State transition of 6.5_KAN for a period	73
Table 6.6	State transition of the 6.5_CON for a period	74
Table 6.7	State transition of 6.6_KAN for a period	82
Table 6.8	State transition of the 6.6_CON for a period	83
Table 6.9	Cycle means in the CONWIP	84
Table 6.10	Cycle means in the Kanban	85
Table 6.11	State transition of 6.7_KAN for a period	90
Table 6.12	State transition of 6.7_BAS for a period	92

Table 6.13	State transition of 6.8_KAN for a period	93
Table 6.14	State transition of 6.8_BAS for a period	95
Table 6.15	State transition of 6.8_CON for a period	96
Table 6.16	Parameters in Examples 6.6, 6.7, and 6.8	97

Notations

a	The notation represents an activity
q	The notation represents a connecting queue
$\|q\|$	The number of tokens in queue q
A	The set of internal activities
E	The set of external activities
Q	The set of queues
C	A circuit
$A(\overline{C})$	The set of activities in a circuit $\overline{C}$
$Q(\overline{C})$	The set of queues in a circuit $\overline{C}$
n_C	The number of tokens in circuit $\overline{C}$
CT_C	The cycle time of circuit $\overline{C}$
λ	Maximum cycle mean
ρ	Activation frequency
L	The time length of a period
TH	Throughput
CT	Cycle time
WIP_A	Average WIP
b	Finished products buffer
M	Raw material
$\mathcal{N}$	The total number of workstations in the system
i, j	Unique number identifying an activity/workstation
p_i	The manufacturing/assembly process of activity i
h_i	The holding time (processing time) of activity i
b_i	The output buffer of workstation i
w_i	The worker//machine/facility of workstation i
K_i	The queue contains workstation i kanbans
k_i	The total number of kanbans in workstation i
$\overline{C}_{ij}$	The outmost circuit ij in CONWIP
C_{ij}	The queue in CONWIP contains conwip cards of circuit $\overline{C}_{ij}$
c_{ij}	The total number of tokens in circuit $\overline{C}_{ij}$
N	The total number of cards in CONWIP
K	The total number of cards in Kanban
B	The total number of cards in Base-stock

h_q	The integration value of tokens in the connecting q for a period
w	The sum of integration values of all activity circuits for a period
W_q^C	The sum of integration values of all connecting queues in CONWIP for a period
W_q^K	The sum of integration values of all connecting queues in Kanban for a period
W_q^B	The sum of integration values of all connecting queues in Base-stock for a period
W_C	The average system WIP in CONWIP
W_K	The average system WIP in Kanban
W_B	The average system WIP in Base-stock

Introduction

Production management deals with planning, organizing, coordinating, and controlling the activities required to make a product. It involves having an effective control over resources, cost, quality, scheduling, and performance. Production control is the function of management which plans, directs, and controls the material supply and processing activities through the entire production cycle. It plays a key role in the success or failure of any corporation. Effective control systems are necessary in any manufacturing firm desiring to maintain a high service level with minimum inventory at a minimum cost. Production control systems that control material flow and inventory are therefore necessary for balancing such objectives.

Systems used for production control can be categorized as push, pull, or hybrid depending on the type of planning strategy they utilize. The focus of this book is on analyzing three pull production control systems, Kanban, Constant work-in-process (CONWIP), and Base-stock, and comparing their performance in make-to-order (MTO) manufacturing environments.

Although there is much literature on pull control systems, few comprehensive comparative studies exist. This is partly due to the fact that different systems have been described within different frameworks. This book presents a unified framework for performance analysis and comparison among pull production control systems. Three control systems - Kanban, CONWIP, and Base-stock - are analyzed and a guideline is provided to choose a proper one in production processes to achieve better performance. By employing a proper control system the maximum possible throughput of the production system with the minimum WIP inventory can be achieved. Analytical comparisons among the three pull control systems are presented in both serial and assembly production processes.

Kanban as a well-known pull production control system was first developed and practiced in Toyota as an important part of Toyota production system. This chapter gives a brief overview of Toyota production system and its core concepts.

1.1 Toyota Production Systems

The Toyota Production System (TPS) was developed and promoted by Toyota Motor Corporation, which is being adopted by many companies. The main purpose of the TPS is to make products with effective tools and techniques to maximize profit. To achieve this purpose, the primary goal of the TPS is cost reduction as well as productivity improvement. Costs include not only manufacturing cost, but also costs related to sales, administration, and capital. The elimination of waste is the way the TPS plans to reduce costs. *Waste* (*muda* in Japanese) is anything that does not add value to the product or service from the customer point of view.

Monden (2011) classified waste in manufacturing production operations in four levels.

1. Excessive production resources
2. Overproduction
3. Excessive inventory
4. Unnecessary capital investment

The primary waste is the existence of *excessive production resources* such as excessive workforce, excessive facilities, and excessive inventory. Excessive workforce leads to unnecessary personnel costs, excessive facilities to unnecessary depreciation costs, and excessive inventory (in the form of raw material, work-in-process, finished goods, etc.) to unnecessary inventory holding costs. Moreover, holding those excessive resources can lead the management to fully use those resources when it is not needed which causes the secondary waste: *overproduction*. Overproduction is to continue working when it is not required by the market. This causes the third type of waste: *excessive inventory*, which requires more manpower, more equipment, and more floor space to store and manage it. This causes the forth type of waste, *unnecessary capital*, which can bring to several costs such as the cost of building a new warehouse to store extra inventory, cost of hiring extra workers for transportation, and also for managing the inventory. Management must focus mostly on the primary wastes to avoid the others (Monden 2011).

Types of waste can be classified differently as follows (Ohno 1988; Liker 2004).

- *Overproduction*: Producing more than the customer orders, or producing early (before it is demanded).
- *Queues/waiting*: Waiting for material, information, equipment, tools, etc.; also, idle times (man waiting for machine, or machine/materials waiting for man).
- *Transportation*: Moving material between plants or between work centers and handling more than once.
- *Over processing*: Effort such as reworking which adds no value to a product or service. A tool called "value stream mapping" (VSM) can be used to help identify over processing steps in the process (for both manufacturers and service sectors).
- *Inventory*: Unnecessary raw material, work in process, and finished goods.

- *Motion*: Unnecessary movement of equipment or people which is caused by poor workflow, poor layout, housekeeping, and inconsistent or undocumented work methods. VSM can also be used to identify this type of waste.
- *Defective product*: Returns, warranty claims, rework, and scrap are waste.

Ohno (1988) described two key concepts of *just-in-time* and *autonomation* as two pillars to support the TPS. The following two sections describe these two concepts.

1.2 Just-In-Time Systems

Just-in-time (JIT) is Toyota's philosophy of minimizing waste. JIT is a set of principles, tools, and techniques that allows a company to produce and deliver products in small quantities, with short lead times to meet specific customer needs. It is an inventory strategy to increase efficiency and decrease work-in-process (WIP) inventory, thereby reducing inventory costs.

JIT basically means to produce the necessary parts in the necessary quantities at the necessary time. That is, only specifically requested items in the right quantity move through the production system when they are needed. Supplying what is needed, when it is needed, and in the right quantity can eliminate waste, inconsistencies, and unreasonable requirements, resulting in improved productivity. Through this method, Toyota successfully discovered a way to eliminate waste to reach the ultimate goal of reducing production time and costs.

JIT flow requires a very smoothly operation system. If materials are not available when a workstation requires them, the entire system may be disrupted. If JIT is realized in the entire firm, then unnecessary inventories in the factory will be completely eliminated making warehouses unnecessary (Monden 2011).

1.2.1 JIT Goals

The goals of JIT can be described in terms of the seven zeros to achieve zero inventories (Edwards 1983; Hopp and Spearman 2008):

- *Zero defects*: to avoid disruptions of the production process due to defects
- *Zero lot size*: to replenish the storage of all parts quickly enough to avoid delays
- *Zero setups*: to lower setups to achieve small lot sizes
- *Zero breakdowns*: to avoid halting whole production line
- *Zero handling*: to avoid extra moves to and from storage
- *Zero lead time*: to have a perfect parts flow providing required parts to a downstream station immediately
- *Zero surging*: to avoid unnecessary work-in-process buffers

Two main concepts are embodied in JIT: *kaizen* (continuous improvement), and inventory reduction. JIT emphasizes inventory reduction. Indeed, it sees inventory as an evil in many aspects. First, inventory is an investment; it has a financial cost that affects price competitiveness. Second, it is used to hide problems such as poor quality of products, process inefficiencies (machine breakdowns, long set-up times, large batch sizes, etc.), inefficient layout, unreliable supplier, difficulties respect to due dates, etc.

Often, people working on JIT use the metaphor of a company floating as a boat on a sea of inventory. Lowering the sea (inventory) level uncovers rocks (problems). The idea emphasized by the JIT philosophy is that the sea level should be gradually lowered, and uncovered rocks should be removed. The JIT technique for lowering inventory is pull production (such as Kanban system), and the technique for removing rocks is continuous improvement. See Imai (1986, 2012) for continuous improvement (kaizen) concepts and applications.

In this book, we focus only on inventory reduction aspect of the JIT, especially WIP inventory by addressing pull production control systems. WIP is the inventory between the start and end points of a product routing in a production process.

In addition to JIT system, Toyota employ the autonomation (*Jidohka* in Japanese) introduced by Ohno as a part of TPS. Autonomation supports JIT by never allowing defective parts from a proceeding process to flow into and disrupt a subsequent process. That is, machines will stop automatically whenever a problem occurs (Monden 2011). At Toyota, for instance, all machines are equipped with automatic stop mechanisms. Each time a defective item is produced, the machine stops immediately and the entire line shuts down. A through adjustment must be made to prevent the recurrence of the same mistake.

1.3 Objectives

Selecting a suitable production control system is a challenging task for managers because the superiority of one control over the other is controversial. According to the survey done by Framinan et al. (2003), the comparison results among the three pull control systems – Kanban, CONWIP, and Base-stock - seem to be contradictory in the literature. They recommended further research to clarify the apparently contradictory results. This is the main reason that we chose only those three control systems for analysis.

This book aims to develop a unified framework for analyzing and comparing performance of pull production control systems. The book provides a guideline to choose a proper control system in production processes to achieve better performance.

By means of the theory of token transaction systems, analytical comparisons among the three pull control systems are presented in both multi-stage serial and assembly production processes. The results show which structural parameters decide the superiority of one control scheme to the others, and how they are related.

We first analyze Kanban, CONWIP, and Base-stock, and present comparative results among them in serial production lines having two or more workstations. Then, we provide analytical comparative results of those control systems in assembly production processes. We examine two different production logistic processes, serial and assembly production processes.

1.4 Structure of the Book

This book is organized as follows. Chapter 2 gives an overview of production systems including pull and push systems, and highlights the key distinctions between them. Chapter 3 describes the characteristics and dynamics of various types of control policies including some hybrid controls. In Chap. 4, the concept of token transaction systems and related definitions are briefly introduced. The properties of token transaction systems that are used in the analysis are also provided in this chapter. In Chap. 5, Kanban, CONWIP, and Base-stock are analyzed, and comparative results among them in serial production lines are presented. In Chap. 6, analytical results of comparison among Kanban, CONWIP, and Base-stock are provided in assembly production processes. Chapter 7 discusses the conclusions drawn from the analysis and experiments, and outlines the suggestions for future studies in this field.

The structure of the book is summarized in Fig. 1.1.

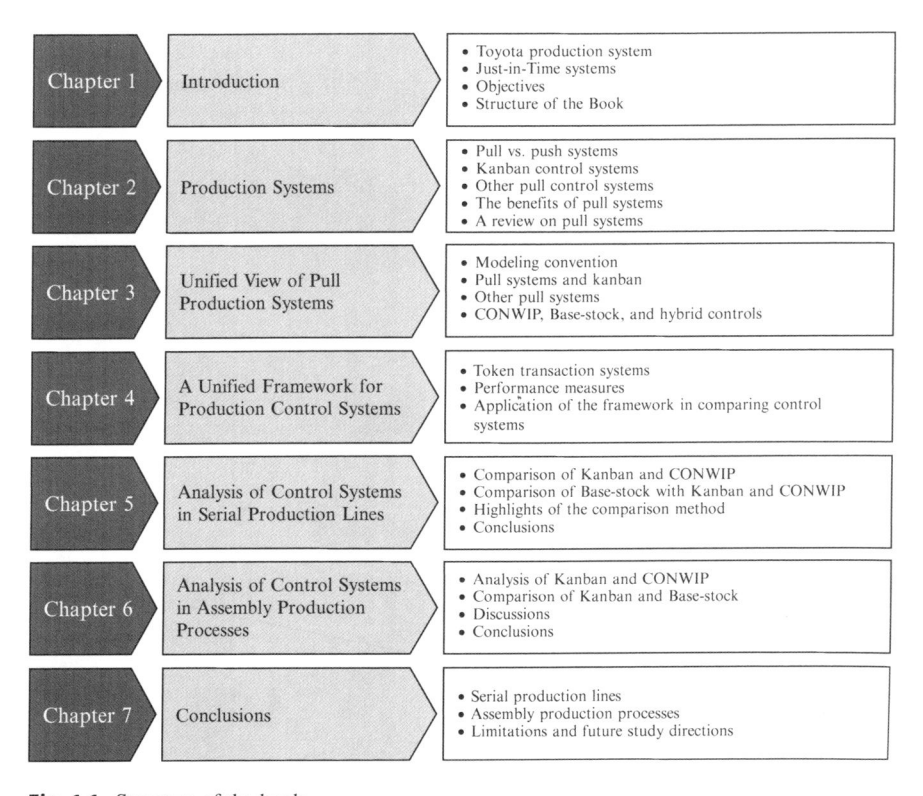

Chapter 1	Introduction	• Toyota production system • Just-in-Time systems • Objectives • Structure of the Book
Chapter 2	Production Systems	• Pull vs. push systems • Kanban control systems • Other pull control systems • The benefits of pull systems • A review on pull systems
Chapter 3	Unified View of Pull Production Systems	• Modeling convention • Pull systems and kanban • Other pull systems • CONWIP, Base-stock, and hybrid controls
Chapter 4	A Unified Framework for Production Control Systems	• Token transaction systems • Performance measures • Application of the framework in comparing control systems
Chapter 5	Analysis of Control Systems in Serial Production Lines	• Comparison of Kanban and CONWIP • Comparison of Base-stock with Kanban and CONWIP • Highlights of the comparison method • Conclusions
Chapter 6	Analysis of Control Systems in Assembly Production Processes	• Analysis of Kanban and CONWIP • Comparison of Kanban and Base-stock • Discussions • Conclusions
Chapter 7	Conclusions	• Serial production lines • Assembly production processes • Limitations and future study directions

Fig. 1.1 Structure of the book

References

Edwards, J. N. (1983). MRP and Kanban – American Style. *APICS 26th conference proceedings*, pp. 586–603.

Framinan, J. M., Gonzalez, P. L., & Ruiz-Usano, R. (2003). The CONWIP production control system: Review and research issues. *Production Planning and Control, 14*, 255–265.

Hopp, W. J., & Spearman, M. L. (2008). *Factory physics* (3rd ed.). New York: McGraw-Hill.

Imai, M. (1986). *Kaizen: The key to Japan's competitive success*. New York: McGraw Hill.

Imai, M. (2012). *Gemba Kaizen: A commonsense approach to a continuous improvement strategy* (2nd ed.). New York: McGraw Hill.

Liker, J. K. (2004). *The Toyota way: 14 management principles from the world's greatest manufacturer*. New York: McGraw-Hill.

Monden, Y. (2011). *Toyota production system: An integrated approach to just-in-time* (4th ed.). Boca Raton, FL: CRC Press

Ohno, T. (1988). *Toyota production system: Beyond large scale production*. Cambridge, MA: Productivity Press.

Production Systems 2

Production systems can be categorized as push, pull and hybrid, depending on the type of planning strategy they utilize. This chapter aims to give an overview of two main production systems, push and pull, and to highlight the key differences between them. A literature review on pull production control systems is also presented at the end of the chapter.

2.1 Pull vs. Push Systems

2.1.1 The Key Differences Between Push and Pull

What distinguishes push from pull is the mechanism that triggers the movement of work in the system. Fundamentally, the trigger for work releases comes from *outside* of a push system but from *inside* a pull system. As a definition, push systems *schedule* work releases on the basis of information from outside the system, while pull systems *authorize* releases based on information from inside the system. That is, a push system *schedules* the release of work based on demand, while a pull system *authorizes* the release of work based on system status. Therefore, push systems schedule periodic releases of raw materials into the production line, while pull systems authorize parts to be processed in response to the actual demand arrival. The difference is that a schedule is prepared in advance, while an authorization depends on the status of the plant (Hopp and Spearman 2008).

Because a pull system controls the releases of row materials and parts into the system, there will be a limit on the maximum level of inventory in the system. This is controlled by using cards or signals that authorize releases of parts into the system. Therefore, in a pull system, WIP level cannot exceed the prespecified limit. However, in a push system, there is no control on part releases since they are based on a predetermined schedule.

Since the term pull production is widely used in recent publications and literature, it may contribute to confusion to think that pull systems are modern production systems while push ones are those of traditional production systems. In fact, the production system is mainly decided by the nature of the product and the customer ordering system. If a product is made based on an actual order from the outside of the plant (customer), the production system can be a pull-based system. A good example of companies employing pull systems is most car manufacturers, where customers can order a car with different design features among many available options. However, a push system is required to produce standard products in high quantities. In such a system, production order is basically based on forecasting demand for a year or so. Therefore, forecasting demand is a main input for push systems in order to develop master production schedules and material requirements plans.[1] Productions of standard products such as TV, bulb-lamp, paper, pen, etc., are among examples that require a push production system.

Moreover, it should be noted that pull production is different from *lean* production. Pull is essentially a mechanism for limiting WIP, but lean is fundamentally about minimizing the cost of buffering variability. Production of goods or services is lean if it is accomplished with minimal buffering costs (Hopp and Spearman 2004).

See Spearman et al. (1990), Spearman and Zazanis (1992), Hopp and Spearman (2004, 2008) for advantages of the pull systems over the push systems.

2.2 Push Systems

The push production systems meet customer's requirement based on forecasted demand. Companies must predict the types of products and quantity of each to be purchased by customers. Therefore, forecasting demand is a crucial input for push systems. Assume that forecast for a specific product is 10,000 units for the next year. This leads to have the daily production schedule of 40 units assuming that the company operates based on 250 working days per year. In order to produce 40 products a day, all raw materials and components required to produce this number of products are gradually released into the line/system, and then they are pushed along the line to become finished products. At the end of the day, 40 products will be delivered to the finished goods warehouse, distribution centers, or customers.

A main input for push systems is forecasting demand. A disadvantage of push systems is that forecasts are often inaccurate as sales can be unpredictable and vary from one period to the next. Therefore, if a huge amount of products are left in inventory because of forecasting errors, then the inventory costs will increase.

Prominent implementations using mainly the push system are material requirements planning (MRP) systems. The following sections describe MRP systems and provides an example for illustration.

---

[1] More details about these concepts will be provided later in this chapter.

2.2.1 MRP

MRP was developed in the early 1960s by Joseph Orlicky (1975) as computer technology started to be used commonly by companies. The basic function of MRP is to determine quantities and process start times for intermediate products (or ordering times for raw materials) based on actual or forecasted demands for final products. Its purpose is to ensure availability of raw materials and components for planned production while maintaining the lowest possible level of inventory.

MRP is useful for *dependent demand* items. Demand for items are dependent when the relationship between the items can be determined. That is, given a quantity for the end item, the demand for all parts and components can be calculated. In fact, demand for end items (finished products) are independent, while demand for components used to manufacture end items are dependent. For example, suppose demand for a bicycle consisting of two wheels and a frame along with other parts is 100 units per day. Then, demand for frame would also be 100 per day, and demand for wheels would be 200 per day. Demand of wheels is totally *dependent* on the demand for bicycles. The demand for bicycles may be forecasted, but the demand for wheels is calculated. The bicycle is an example of independent demand, and the frame and wheels are examples of dependent demands.

Figure 2.1 shows the inputs to and outputs from the MRP system. The three major inputs are the *master production schedule*, the *bill of material*, and the *inventory data*. Without these basic inputs the MRP system cannot function. The main output of the system is *planned order releases* for all items and components. That is, it determines the quantity and timing of placing orders to purchase row material, or to start production of an item. Basic inputs for the MRP are described below.

Master Production Schedule

Master production schedule (MPS) specifies which finished products are to be made and when. This schedule must be in accordance with the aggregate production plan (APP). An APP determines the quantity and timing of production for a family of products for a year or per month. The plan is developed by the sales and operations planning (SOP) department based on forecasts for independent demand.

Breaking the aggregate plan down, or *disaggregation*, results in MPS. So, MPS is derived from the aggregate plan.

Table 2.1 shows the master production schedule for three LCD TV types that flow from the aggregate plan for a family of LCD TVs. It shows that the schedule in January is to produce 5000 LCD TVs out of which 2400 are 32-inch, 2000 are 42-inch, and the rest are 46-inch types. 32-inch models should be produced in weeks 2 and 4 and 1200 units in each week, 1000 units of 42-inch should be produced in each of weeks 1 and 3, and 600 units of 46-inch in week 3. Similarly, February schedule is to produce 3500 LCD TVs out of which 1700 are 32-inch, 1400 are 42-inch, and 400 are 46-inch types. 32-inch models should be produced in weeks 6 and 8 and 850 units in each week, 700 units of 42-inch in each of weeks 5 and 7, and 400 units of 46-inch in week 6.

Fig. 2.1 Material requirements planning

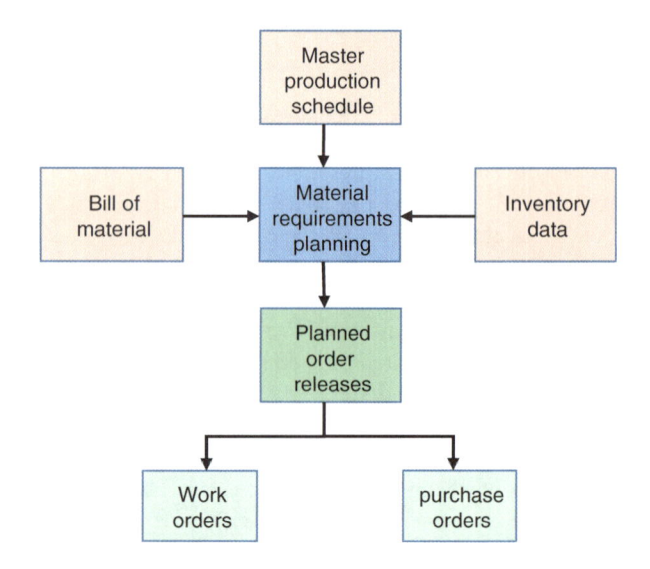

Table 2.1 Master production schedule based on an aggregate plan

Months	January				February			
Aggregate production plan	5,000				3,500			
Weeks	1	2	3	4	5	6	7	8
Master production schedule								
LCD TV 32"		1200		1200		850		850
LCD TV 42"	1000		1000		700		700	
LCD TV 46"			600			400		

Bill of Material

The bill of material (BOM) is a list of items/components required to produce a finished product. It shows the structure of a product which includes a brief description of each item, and the quantity of each required to make one unit of the product. Moreover, lead times[2] of the finished product and all components must be known.

Example 2.1 A BOM for a product is depicted in Fig. 2.2. It shows that product A consists of items B and C. Two units of item B and one unit of item C are required to produce one unit of product A. One unit of item B requires three units of item D, one unit of item E, and two units of item F. Also, one unit of item C requires three units of item E.

In a BOM, items above any level are called *parents*, and items below any level are called *components* or *children*. By convention, the top level in a BOM is the zero level.

---

[2] Lead time of a product is the time needed to assemble it, assuming that all required components are available.

Fig. 2.2 A bill of material

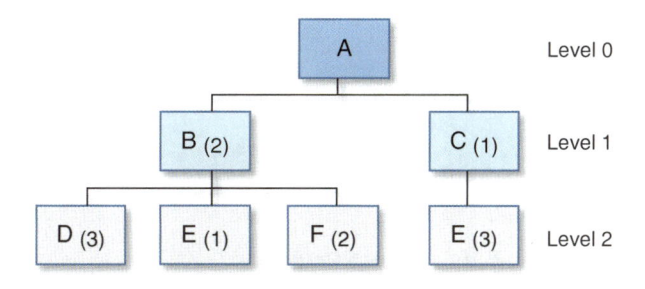

```
                    A                Level 0
                   / \
                 B(2)  C(1)          Level 1
                /|\     |
              D(3) E(1) F(2)  E(3)   Level 2
```

In the above example, suppose further that the lead time for the items A, B, C, D, E, and F is 2, 3, 1, 2, 1, and 2 days, respectively as shown in Table 2.2. This means that, for example, it takes 3 days to assemble one unit of item B given that its components (namely, three of item D, one of item E, and two of item F) are available.

Given the demand for the finished product, the number of required units of each item/component can be calculated. Suppose you need to produce 100 units of product A. How many units of each type do you need? Here are the requirements:

Part B: $2 \times$ number of As $= (2)(100) = 200$
Part C: $1 \times$ number of As $= (1)(100) = 100$
Part D: $3 \times$ number of Bs $= (3)(200) = 600$
Part E: $1 \times$ number of Bs $+ 3 \times$ number of Cs $= (1)(200) + (3)(100) = 500$
Part F: $2 \times$ number of Bs $= (2)(200) = 400$

Inventory Data

Inventory data contains the status of all items in inventory, including on-hand inventory, scheduled receipts, and safety stock. On-hand inventory shows what is in stock, but the scheduled receipt shows what is on order. On-hand inventories for the items in Example 2.1 are also shown in Table 2.2.

2.2.1.1 MRP Process

Starting with end items, the MRP process goes through the following steps.

1. Developing gross requirements plan.
2. Determining net requirements plan.
3. Determining the planned order releases.

1. *Gross requirements plan*

Gross requirements plan is a schedule that shows when an item must be ordered from suppliers (if the item is a purchased item), or when the production of an item must be started to satisfy demand for the finished product by a particular date.

Table 2.2 Lead times and on-hand inventories

Item	Lead time (day)	On hand	Item	Lead time (day)	On hand
A	2	10	D	2	60
B	3	15	E	1	35
C	1	5	F	2	30

Table 2.3 A gross requirements plan

		Day 1	2	3	4	5	6	7	8	Lead time
A.	Required date								100	
	Order release date						100			2 days
B.	Required date						200			
	Order release date			200						3 days
C.	Required date						100			
	Order release date					100				1 day
D.	Required date			600						
	Order release date	600								2 days
E.	Required date			200		300				
	Order release date		200		300					1 day
F.	Required date			400						
	Order release date	400								2 days

Table 2.3 shows the gross requirements plan with a production schedule to satisfy the demand of 100 units of Product A on day 8. The BOM and lead times are shown in Fig. 2.2, and Table 2.2, respectively.

The gross requirements plan given in Table 2.3 shows when production of each item should start and end in order to have 100 units of product A available on day 8. To have 100 units of product A on day 8, assembling of A must start on day 6 (because its lead time is 2 days). Thus, on day 6, 200 units of item B and 100 units of item C must be available. These two items require 3 days and 1 day, respectively, to produce. Therefore, production of B must start on day 3 (=6 − 3), and production of item C must start on day 5 (=6 − 1). The start and end dates for the other items can be calculated in the same way.

2. *Net requirements plan*

In developing a gross requirements plan, we assume that there is no inventory on-hand. A net requirements plan is determined by subtracting on-hand inventory and any scheduled receipts from the gross requirements.

Assume that we need to produce 100 units of Product A 8 days from now. In order to develop a net requirements plan, inventory data should be available. Suppose the on-hand inventory of items are those given in Table 2.2. Suppose further that on-order inventory (scheduled receipts) for all items is zero.

2.2 Push Systems

Given the gross requirements plan and the inventory data, a net requirements plan can be developed. The gross requirement for product A is 100 and there are 10 of that product on hand, thus the net requirement for A is 90 (=100 − 10). To determine when to release the order, the lead time is subtracted from the time of plan order receipts. This yields the planned order releases. For product A, an order for 90 As must be placed on day 6 (=8 − 2).

However, each on hand product A contains 2 Bs and one C. As a result, the requirements for B and C items drop by 20 and 10, respectively. Therefore, the updated gross requirements for items B and C are respectively 180 and 90 units in day 6 (lead time of product A is 2 days, meaning that all its components must be available on day 6). Table 2.4 shows net requirements plan for product A and its components.

2.2.1.2 Lot-Sizing Techniques

There are different ways to determine lot sizes in an MRP system. The method used in determining lot sizes is called *lot-sizing method*. The most well-known lot-sizing methods are as follows.

- Lot-for-lot method
- Economic order quantity method
- Periodic order quantity method
- Part-period balancing method
- Wagner-Whitin method.

Lot-for-lot (L4L) method orders exactly what is required. For instance, if the planned order receipt for an item is 50 units, then an order for exactly 50 units will be placed considering the lead time of the item. In the above example (Table 2.4) lot-for-lot method is used to determine the planned order receipts and planned order releases. This method is effective when the setup (ordering) costs are relatively small compared to holding costs.

Economic order quantity (EOQ) method determines the lot sizes using the economic order quantity formula as below.

$$\text{EOQ} = \sqrt{\frac{2DS}{H}},$$

where D is the annual demand, S is the setup (ordering) cost per order, and H is the holding cost per unit per year.

EOQ minimizes the total annual inventory costs which is achieved when the annual holing costs equal annual setup (ordering) costs. This method is more effective when demand is stable over periods. It does not perform well when demand is highly variable.

Table 2.4 Net requirements plan for Product A

Item			Day 1	2	3	4	5	6	7	8
A	Gross requirements									100
	Scheduled receipts									
	Projected on-hand	10	10	10	10	10	10	10	10	10
	Net requirements									90
	Planned order receipts									90
	Planned order releases							90		
B	Gross requirements							180		
	Scheduled receipts									
	Projected on-hand	15	15	15	15	15	15	15		
	Net requirements							165		
	Planned order receipts							165		
	Planned order releases				165					
C	Gross requirements							90		
	Scheduled receipts									
	Projected on-hand	5	5	5	5	5	5	5		
	Net requirements							85		
	Planned order receipts							85		
	Planned order releases						85			
D	Gross requirements					495				
	Scheduled receipts									
	Projected on-hand	60	60	60	60					
	Net requirements					435				
	Planned order receipts					435				
	Planned order releases			435						
E	Gross requirements					165		255		
	Scheduled receipts									
	Projected on-hand	35	35	35	35	35	0	0		
	Net requirements					130		255		
	Planned order receipts					130		255		
	Planned order releases				130		255			
F	Gross requirements					330				
	Scheduled receipts									
	Projected on-hand	30	30	30	30	30				
	Net requirements					300				
	Planned order receipts					300				
	Planned order releases			300						

Periodic order quantity (POQ) method is more suitable when demand is variable. It is calculated by dividing the EOQ by average demand per period over a certain period of time. That is,

$$POQ = \frac{EOQ}{\bar{d}},$$

where $\bar{d}$ is average demand per period.

POQ represents the number of demand periods covered by each order. For example, if POQ is two, then an order will be placed for two periods worth of demand.

Part-period balancing (PPB) method is a dynamic approach to balance ordering and holding costs by changing the lot size to reflect requirements of the next lot size in the future. PPB is performed by determining the economic part period (EPP), which is the ratio of setup cost to holding cost.

Wagner-Whitin method developed by Wagner and Whitin in 1958 is an algorithm based on dynamic programming principles to make optimal lot size decisions.

2.3 Pull Systems

Pull production systems begin with a customer's order. With this strategy, companies only make enough products to fulfill customer's orders. Therefore, there will be no excess of inventory that needs to be stored, thus reducing inventory levels and holding cost.

Notice that pull production is different from *lean* production. Hopp and Spearman (2004) defined the terms pull and lean production precisely in order to avoid confusion. Pull is essentially a mechanism for limiting WIP, but lean is fundamentally about minimizing the cost of buffering variability. Production of goods or services is lean if it is accomplished with minimal buffering costs.

An ultimate goal of a pull production system is to keep inventory levels to a minimum by only having enough inventory, no more or less, to meet customer demand. A pull production *control* system is then used to control the inventory level, specially WIP inventory. A well-known pull production control system is Kanban which is described in the following section.

2.4 Kanban Control Systems

The word *kanban* is Japanese for *card*. The Kanban control is a system that controls the production quantities in every process. It limits the amount of inventory to a fixed maximum for each workstation consisting of a process and its output buffer, where the maximum is equal to the number of kanbans circulating within the workstation.

In the Kanban system, production is triggered by a demand. When a part is removed from an inventory point (which may be finished goods inventory or some intermediate buffer) the workstation that feeds the inventory point is given authorization to replace the part. This workstation then sends an authorization card/signal to the upstream workstation to replace the part it just used. Each workstation does the same thing, replenishing the downstream void and sending authorization to the next workstation upstream. Therefore, production authorization cards, called kanbans, are used to control and limit the release of parts into each workstation (Hopp and Spearman 2008).

2.4.1 Types of Kanbans and Kanban Rules

The Kanban system developed at Toyota made use of two types of cards to authorize production and movement of product: a withdrawal Kanban and a production-ordering Kanban. A *withdrawal* Kanban specifies the kind and quantity of product which the subsequent process should withdraw from the preceding process, while a *production-ordering* Kanban specifies the kind and quantity of product which the preceding process must produce. The production-ordering Kanban is often called an in-process Kanban or simply a production Kanban (Monden 2011).

The key controls in a Kanban system are the WIP limits at each workstation. These take the form of a card count, a limit on the number of containers, or, simply, a volume limitation.

In a Kanban system, instead of directly controlling the throughput, kanbans (cards) are used to authorize production or transportation of materials such that the parts are pulled and WIP is visualized and controlled. The constant number of cards used in a Kanban system, and the limited lot sizes of the attached containers create an upper limit on the WIP level and the finished good inventory (Akturk and Erhun 1999).

In a Kanban system the following rules must be followed:

1. Downstream workstations should only withdraw parts/containers in the precise amounts specified on the kanban.
2. Upstream workstations should only send parts/containers to downstream workstation in the precise amounts and sequences specified by the kanban.
3. A kanban must always be attached to each part/container.
4. No parts/containers are made or moved without a kanban.
5. Defective parts are never sent to the next downstream workstation.
6. The number of kanbans should be kept as small as possible (because it determines the maximum inventory of a part).

2.4.2 The General Method to Determine the Number of Kanbans

The general formula to determine the number of withdrawal kanbans is as follows.

$$\text{Number of kanbans (containers)} = \frac{\text{Expected demand during lead time} + \text{Safety stock}}{\text{Container capacity}}$$

This can be also expressed as in the following formula.

$$K = \frac{DL(1+s)}{C}$$

where,

K: number of kanbans (containers)
D: demand per time unit
L: lead time
C: container capacity
s: safety stock factor

The safety stock factor in the above formula is expressed as a percentage of demand during lead time. For instance, it is less than 10 % in Toyota.

Example 2.2 Suppose that daily demand is for 200 units, lead time is 6 days, and the container capacity is 60 units. Assume that lead time or daily demand or both are variable, and the safety stock factor is set to 10 %. Then, number of kanbans is determined as follows.

$$K = \frac{DL(1+s)}{C} = \frac{(200)(6)(1+0.1)}{60} = 22$$

In this formula, if the policy is no safety stock ($s=0$), and a container size of 1 ($C=1$), then the number of kanbans will be equal to the expected demand during lead time (DL), which shows the philosophy of the JIT system.

2.5 Other Pull Control Systems

2.5.1 Base-Stock Control System

The Base-stock is another pull control system which has been originated from inventory control technique. It was initially proposed for production/inventory systems with infinite production capacity. The Base-stock control system uses the idea of a safety stock for finished goods inventory as well as safety buffers between workstations for coordination.

Base-stock control system limits the amount of inventory between each production stage and the demand process. It tries to maintain a certain amount of WIP in each stage. This amount is called the *basestock level* of each stage. In other words, the basestock level of a production stage determines the maximum planned inventory of the outputs of the stage (Lee and Zipkin 1992). To operate a Base-stock, it is necessary to transmit demand information to all production stages as demand occurs. An advantage of this mechanism over Kanban is that it avoids demand information blockage by transferring the demand information immediately to all production stages. The down side is that it provides no limit on the number of parts in the system (Kimball 1988).

2.5.2 CONWIP Control System

Constant work-in-process (CONWIP) control system proposed by Spearman et al. (1990) is another pull control system. It uses a single card type to control the total amount of WIP permitted in the entire line. It is a generalization of the Kanban system and can be viewed as a single-stage Kanban system.

In a production line controlled by CONWIP, raw materials are only released into the line if there is an available CONWIP card. No part can enter the line without an attached CONWIP card. As a result, the WIP in the entire line remains constant at the level set by the number of CONWIP cards. Once a part at the beginning of the line is released into the line, it is pushed through the line as fast as possible.

In a CONWIP system, the release sequence of jobs is given by a *release list*, with actual releases occurring only when authorized by a CONWIP card. The release list is one important mechanism for linking output from a CONWIP line with customer demand.

2.5.3 Hybrid Control Systems

Other than the basic pull control systems, there are some hybrid controls which are combinations of two basic control systems. For instance, Buzacott (1989) proposed a hybrid control system, called *Generalized Kanban control system (GKCS)*, which combines the Kanban and Base-stock control systems. It depends on two parameters per production stage, the basestock level of the finished parts, and the number of kanbans.

Extended Kanban control system (EKCS) is another hybrid control system introduced by Dallery and Liberopoulos (2000). Same as the GKCS, it combines the Kanban and Base-stock control systems; however, this is conceptually less complicated that the Generalized Kanban system.

Another hybrid control is *CONWIP-Kanban* system. This control system combines WIP control mechanism at each stage using kanbans and the inventory control in the entire system using CONWIP cards. Demand information is transferred to the first stage using CONWIP mechanism. However, this information flow can still be halted if there is no finished goods inventory at the time demand arrives.

The three basic control systems along with the hybrid CONWIP-Kanban are more illustrated in Chap. 3.

Hereafter, we simply write Kanban, CONWIP, and Base-stock to mean respective Kanban, CONWIP, and Base-stock controlled production processes, as long as it is clear from the context.

2.6 The Benefits of Pull Systems

Pull production systems provide a wide range of benefits. The benefits can be easily seen and felt in a best practice operation. This is because of the simple but powerful concept of pull systems: produce only what the customer (or next step) wants, when the customer (next step) wants it.

The benefits include:

- Reduced inventory, and hence lower inventory holding costs
- Shorter lead time (the time it takes for customers to get what they requested)
- Shorter time to detect errors and quality problems (because of a lower level of WIP)
- Less handling damage and lower material handling costs (because of a lower level of WIP)
- Reduced space requirements
- Reduced manufacturing costs
- Reduced set-up time and response time
- Easier control of WIP
- Less variability
- Improved quality
- Increased productivity
- Simplified scheduling and control activities
- Greater flexibility
- Better relations with suppliers

2.7 A Review on Pull Systems

There are many studies on control mechanisms for manufacturing systems. However, we consider the studies that mainly address comparisons among Kanban, CONWIP, and Base-stock. (See, for example, Berkley (1992) for a survey paper on Kanban, and Framinan et al. (2003) for a survey paper on CONWIP. Also, see for example, Spearman et al. (1990), Hopp and Roof (1998), Huang et al. (1998), Duri et al. (2000b), Framinan et al. (2000), Zhang and Chen (2001), Ip et al. (2007), Yildiz and Tunali (2008) on the application of CONWIP in manufacturing systems, and Hopp and Spearman (1991), Duenyas and Hopp (1992, 1993), Duenyas (1994), and Hazra and Seidmann (1996) for its application in assembly operations.)

Sato and Khojasteh-Ghamari (2012) developed an integrated framework for analyzing performance of card-based production control mechanisms using the theory of token transaction systems. Khojasteh-Ghamari (2012) proposed a model for performance analysis of a production process controlled by Kanban and CONWIP. He showed that initial inventories as well as card distribution are important parameters that influence the system performance.

Liberopoulos and Dallery (2000) presented a unified framework for pull production control mechanisms in serial production lines. They used the framework to model the operation of four basic pull production control mechanisms, Base-stock, Kanban, Generalized Kanban, and Extended Kanban in a serial production line. Bollon et al. (2004) proposed a unified formulation based on (min, +) algebra to express the dynamics of pull control mechanisms for serial single product manufacturing systems. With the proposed formulation, they examined the dynamics behavior of Kanban, Base-stock, Extended Kanban, and Generalized Kanban. Di Mascolo and Bollon (2011) presented a framework to describe the dynamics of pull control mechanisms using (max, +) algebra.

In a survey paper, Framinan et al. (2003) reviewed comparison of CONWIP with other production control mechanisms. Bonvik et al. (1997), Bonvik and Gershwin (1996), Paternina-Arboleda and Das (2001), and Yang (2000) used simulation for analysis of performance of different production control mechanisms in serial production processes. Spearman and Zazanis (1992) and Muckstadt and Tayur (1995) showed analytical result on card-based control for serial production processes. When the same number of cards is used in both CONWIP and Kanban, Spearman and Zazanis (1992) showed that CONWIP produces a higher mean throughput than Kanban. In the same scenario, Muckstadt and Tayur (1995) considered, simultaneously, four sources of variability in production lines – processing time variability, machine breakdowns, rework, and yield loss – and showed some similarities and differences in their effects on the performance of the line. They showed that CONWIP produces a less variable throughput and a lower maximal inventory than Kanban.

Sharma and Agrawal (2009) implemented an analytic hierarchy process (AHP) algorithm to compare CONWIP, Kanban, and Hybrid with respect to average utilization of machine and buffer, service level, WIP, throughput, unsatisfied demand, and total cost in a serial production line with four workstations. They considered four probabilistic situations – binomial, exponential, lognormal, and Poisson – for the demand. They showed that the Kanban is superior to the CONWIP with the binomial, exponential, and Poisson demands, and CONWIP is the superior with the lognormal demand.

Gaury et al. (2000) compared Kanban, CONWIP, and hybrid in a serial production line having six, eight, and ten workstations. Their methodology is based on optimization, using an evolutionary algorithm, and discrete-event simulation. They pointed out that the hybrid control mechanism has the best performance among those three control mechanisms.

2.7 A Review on Pull Systems

Lödding (2013) and Huang et al. (2013) addressed hybrid Kanban-CONWIP control system and conducted some simulation studies to evaluate the system performance. Renna et al. (2013) presented a dynamic card control methodology in pull production systems, and conducted simulation studies to test their proposed methodology in Kanban and CONWIP control systems.

Pettersen and Segerstedt (2009) compared Kanban and CONWIP through a simulation study over a small supply chain, which consists of five linked machines with stochastic operation times. They showed that with the same amount of limited WIP, the CONWIP control is superior to the Kanban with a higher throughput rate and a lower time between jobs.

According to the survey done by Framinan et al. (2003), in comparison of CONWIP and Kanban, many authors have shown through both simulation and analytical models that CONWIP outperforms Kanban when processing times on component operations in production processes are variable. However, Gstettner and Kuhn (1996) and Khojasteh-Ghamari (2009) arrived at the opposite conclusion. According to their results, Kanban achieves a given throughput level with a small amount of WIP. They showed that by choosing an appropriate number of cards at each workstation, Kanban can outperform the CONWIP.

There are also some studies in the literature for comparing Base-stock with the other production control mechanisms. Duri et al. (2000a) compared three production control mechanisms, Kanban, Base-stock, and the Generalized Kanban, in serial production lines with Poisson demand arrival process and exponentially distributed processing times. They showed that if there is no delay in filling orders, all three mechanisms have similar performance; otherwise, the Generalized Kanban and Base-stock systems outperform Kanban with a lower cost and the same service quality. Also, using simulation analysis, Bonvik et al. (1997) compared the performance of different production control mechanisms with respect to WIP and service level in a serial production line with four workstations. They showed that CONWIP demonstrates superior performance in achieving a high service level target with minimal WIP, followed by Base-stock and Kanban. However, as Framinan et al. (2003) mentioned, this result seems to be contradictory to the findings of Duenyas and Patana-anake (1998) and Paternina-Arboleda and Das (2001), which indicated that Base-stock outperforms CONWIP in a serial production line. Framinan et al. (2003) recommended further research to clarify these apparently contradictory results.

Takahashi et al. (2005) applied Kanban, CONWIP, and synchronized CONWIP to supply chains to determine the superior system. Their considered supply chains contain assembly stages with different lead times, and a sufficient production capacity at each process. Their simulation results show the superiority of both CONWIP and synchronized CONWIP over Kanban, when all inventory levels among the stages are equally important. However, we have no knowledge of papers in the literature that address Base-stock control system in a non-serial production line to analyze the system performance.

See Geraghty and Heavey (2006) and Gonzlez-R et al. (2012) for more review of the literature for comparison of pull control systems.

References

Akturk, M. S., & Erhun, F. (1999). An overview of design and operational issues of Kanban systems. *International Journal of Production Research, 37*, 3859–3881.
Berkley, B. J. (1992). A review of the kanban production control research literature. *Production and Operations Management, 1*(4), 393–411.
Bollon, J.-M., Di Mascolo, M., & Frein, Y. (2004). Unified framework for describing comparing the dynamics of pull control policies. *Annals of Operations Research, 125*, 21–45.
Bonvik, A. M., & Gershwin, S. B. (1996). Beyond Kanban: Creating and analyzing lean shop floor control policies. In *Manufacturing and service operations management conference proceeding* (pp. 46–51). Hannover: Durtmouth College, The Amos Tuck School.
Bonvik, A. M., Couch, C. E., & Gershwin, S. B. (1997). A comparison of production-line control mechanisms. *International Journal of Production Research, 35*(3), 789–804.
Buzacott, J. A. (1989). Queuing models of kanban and MRP controlled production systems. *Engineering Cost and Production Economics, 17*, 3–20.
Dallery, Y., & Liberopoulos, G. (2000). Extended kanban control system: Combining kanban and base stock. *IIE Transactions, 32*, 369–386.
Di Mascolo, M., & Bollon, J.-M. (2011). Use of path algebra tools for a unified description of a large class of pull control policies. *International Journal of Production Research, 49*(3), 611–636.
Duenyas, I. (1994). Estimating the throughput of acyclic assembly system. *International Journal of Production Research, 32*, 1403–1419.
Duenyas, I., & Hopp, W. J. (1992). CONWIP assembly with deterministic processing and random outages. *IIE Transactions, 24*, 97–109.
Duenyas, I., & Hopp, W. J. (1993). Estimating the throughput of an exponential CONWIP assembly system. *Queuing Systems, 14*, 135–157.
Duenyas, I., & Patana-anake, P. (1998). Base-stock control for single product tandem make-to-stock systems. *IIE Transactions, 30*, 31–39.
Duri, C., Frein, Y., & Di Mascolo, M. (2000a). Comparison among three pull control policies: Kanban, base stock, and generalized Kanban. *Annals of Operations Research, 93*, 41–69.
Duri, C., Frein, Y., & Lee, H. S. (2000b). Performance evaluation and design of a CONWIP system with inspections. *International Journal of Production Economics, 64*, 219–229.
Framinan, J. M., Ruiz-Usano, R., & Leisten, R. (2000). Input control and dispatching rules in a dynamic CONWIP flow-shop. *International Journal of Production Research, 38*, 4589–4598.
Framinan, J. M., Gonzalez, P. L., & Ruiz-Usano, R. (2003). The CONWIP production control system: Review and research issues. *Production Planning and Control, 14*, 255–265.
Gaury, E. G. A., Pierreval, H., & Kleijnen, J. P. C. (2000). An evolutionary approach to select a pull system among Kanban. Conwip and Hybrid. *Journal of Intelligent Manufacturing, 11*, 157–167.
Geraghty, J., & Heavey, C. (2006). A review and comparison of hybrid and pull-type production control strategies. In G. Liberopoulos, C. T. Papadopoulos, B. Tan, J. MacGregor Smith, & S. B. Gershwin (Eds.), *Stochastic modeling of manufacturing systems*. Berlin/Heidelberg: Springer.
Gonzlez-R, P. L., Framinan, J. M., & Pierreval, H. (2012). Token-based pull production control systems: An introductory overview. *Journal of Intelligent Manufacturing, 23*(1), 5–22.
Gstettner, S., & Kuhn, H. (1996). Analysis of production control systems kanban and CONWIP. *International Journal of Production Research, 34*(11), 3253–3274.
Hazra, J., & Seidmann, A. (1996). Performance evaluation of closed tree-structured assembly systems. *IIE Transactions, 28*, 591–599.
Hopp, W. J., & Roof, M. L. (1998). Setting WIP levels with statistical throughput control (STC) in CONWIP production lines. *International Journal of Production Research, 36*, 867–882.
Hopp, W. J., & Spearman, M. L. (1991). Throughput of a constant work in process manufacturing line subject to failures. *International Journal of Production Research, 29*, 635–655.

References

Hopp, W. J., & Spearman, M. L. (2004). To pull or not to pull: What is the question? *Manufacturing & Service Operations Management, 6*(2), 133–148.

Hopp, W. J., & Spearman, M. L. (2008). *Factory physics* (3rd ed.). New York: McGraw-Hill.

Huang, M., Wang, D., & Ip, W. H. (1998). Simulation study of CONWIP for a cold rolling plant. *International Journal of Production Economics, 54*, 257–266.

Huang, Y., Kuriger, G. & Chen, F. F. (2013) Simulation studies of hybrid pull systems of kanban and conwip in an assembly line. In A. Azevedo (ed.), *Advances in Sustainable and Competitive Manufacturing Systems.* Cham: Springer International Publishing.

Ip, W. H., Huang, M., Yung, K. L., Wang, D., & Wang, X. (2007). CONWIP based control of a lamp assembly production line. *Journal of Intelligent Manufacturing, 18*(2), 261–271.

Khojasteh-Ghamari, Y. (2009). A performance comparison between Kanban and CONWIP controlled assembly systems. *Journal of Intelligent Manufacturing, 20*(6), 751–760.

Khojasteh-Ghamari, Y. (2012). Developing a framework for performance analysis of a production process controlled by Kanban and CONWIP. *Journal of Intelligent Manufacturing, 23*(1), 61–71.

Kimball, G. (1988). General principles of inventory control. *Journal of Manufacturing and Operations Management, 1*(1), 119–130.

Lee, Y.-J., & Zipkin, P. (1992). Tandem queues with planned inventories. *Operations Research, 40*(5), 936–947.

Liberopoulos, G., & Dallery, Y. (2000). A unified framework for pull control mechanisms in multi-stage manufacturing systems. *Annals of Operations Research, 93*, 325–355.

Lödding, H. (2013). Hybrid Kanban/CONWIP Control. In H. Lödding (Ed.), *Handbook of manufacturing control.* Berlin/Heidelberg: Springer.

Monden, Y. (2011). *Toyota production system: An integrated approach to just-in-time* (4th ed.). Boca Raton, FL: CRC Press.

Muckstadt, J. A., & Tayur, S. R. (1995). A comparison of alternative kanban control mechanisms: I, background and structural results. *IIE Transactions, 27*(1), 140–150.

Orlicky, J. (1975). *Material requirements planning: The new way of life in production and inventory management.* New York: McGraw-Hill.

Paternina-Arboleda, C. D., & Das, T. K. (2001). Intelligent dynamic control policies for serial production lines. *IIE Transactions, 33*(1), 65–77.

Pettersen, J. A., & Segerstedt, A. (2009). Restricted work-in-process: A study of differences between Kanban and CONWIP. *International Journal of Production Economics, 118*(1), 199–207.

Renna, P., Magrino, L., & Zaffina, R. (2013). Dynamic card control strategy in pull manufacturing systems. *International Journal of Computer Integrated Manufacturing, 26*(9), 881–894.

Sato, R., & Khojasteh-Ghamari, Y. (2012). An integrated framework for card-based production control systems. *Journal of Intelligent Manufacturing, 23*(3), 717–731.

Sharma, S., & Agrawal, N. (2009). Selection of a pull production control policy under different demand situations for a manufacturing system by AHP-algorithm. *Computers and Operations Research, 36*, 1622–1632.

Spearman, M. L., & Zazanis, M. A. (1992). Push and pull production systems: Issues and comparisons. *Operations Research, 40*, 521–532.

Spearman, M. L., Woodruff, D. L., & Hopp, W. J. (1990). CONWIP: A pull alternative to Kanban. *International Journal of Production Research, 23*, 879–894.

Takahashi, K., Myreshka, K., & Hirotani, D. (2005). Comparing CONWIP, synchronized CONWIP, and Kanban in complex supply chains. *International Journal of Production Economics, 93–94*, 25–40.

Wagner, H. M., & Whitin, T. (1958). Dynamic version of the economic lot size model. *Management Science, 5*, 89–96.

Yang, K. K. (2000). Managing a flow line with single-Kanban, dual-Kanban or CONWIP. *Production and Operations Management, 9*(4), 349–366.

Yildiz, G., & Tunali, S. (2008). Response surface methodology based simulation optimization of a CONWIP controlled dual resource constrained system. *International Journal of Advanced Manufacturing Technology, 36*, 1051–1060.

Zhang, W., & Chen, M. (2001). A mathematical programming model for production planning using CONWIP. *International Journal of Production Research, 39*(12), 2723–2734.

3. Unified View of Pull Production Systems

The operation and control characteristics of some control policies from basic to hybrid ones are described in this chapter. Basic control policies include Kanban, CONWIP, and Base-stock. The simplest is the CONWIP, which has only a single control parameter for the entire production line, whereas Kanban and Base-stock controls require one control parameter for each production stage. Hybrid control policies include Kanban-CONWIP, Generalized Kanban, and Extended Kanban. Among the hybrid controls, we only describe the simplest one, the CONWIP-Kanban, which requires one control parameter for each production stage and one additional parameter for the entire production line.

3.1 Modeling Convention

Consider a manufacturing system in which the production of parts proceeds in several stages. Each stage is a production (or assembly) inventory system made up of a manufacturing (or assembly) process and an output buffer. The manufacturing/assembling process may consist of a single machine or a subnetwork of several machines. This production system controlled by different control policies are illustrated using activity interaction diagrams.

3.1.1 Activity Interaction Diagram

Activity interaction diagram (AID) is used to show the control dynamics of each control policy.

Definition 3.1 *Activity Interaction Diagram (AID)* (Sato and Praehofer 1997)

An activity interaction diagram is a diagram that has three kinds of components. They are activities, queues, and connecting arrows. Activities should be connected with queues, and vice versa.

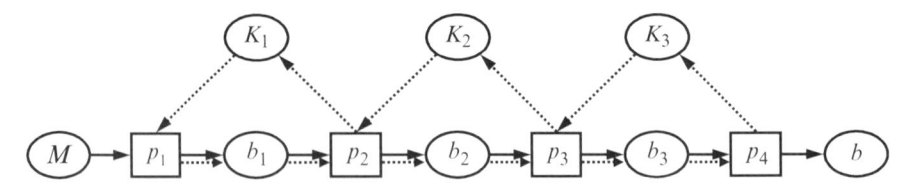

Fig. 3.1 A serial production line controlled by Kanban

The AID for a simple production process is depicted in Fig. 3.1, where activities (processes) and queues (buffers) are represented by squares and ovals, respectively. It shows a serial production line with four workstations governed by Kanban system. The meaning of symbols used in this chapter can be found in the list of notations in Notations list.

In the following sections, the operation and characteristics of pull production control systems are described. For the sake of simplicity, the AID of each control system is shown in a serial production line having four production stages (workstations) in series. A multi-stage system can be modeled based on these four-stage models.

3.2 Pull Systems and Kanban

Kanban control is the most well-known pull production control system which limits the amount of inventory to a fixed maximum for each workstation consisting of a process and its output buffer, where the maximum is equal to the number of kanbans circulating within the workstation.

There are different types of Kanban system, for example, single-card Kanban, two-card Kanban, etc. A comparison of different Kanban systems can be found in Muckstadt and Tayur (1995). We consider only a simple model where information and parts move instantly in batches of one, where there is only one part type, and where the transfer of parts from the output buffer of the preceding station follows the "late material transfer" (LMT) policy. Under this policy, when information about a demand arrives at a workstation, the material is not taken from the preceding buffer until the station is ready to start production (Gstettner and Kuhn 1996). That is, the machine does not load a new part from upstream when the downstream buffer is full, and remains empty until material is removed from the downstream buffer.

Figure 3.1 shows the AID of a simple Kanban system having four workstations in series. For consistency purpose, we depicted the system with four workstations, and the other control policies which will be described later are also depicted with four workstations. The manufacturing/assembling processes at each workstation are drawn as squares and buffers as ovals. M represents raw material buffer, and b represents the finished products buffer. Queue K_i contains station i kanbans.

Queue b_i is the output buffer of station i containing both finished parts and the kanbans of station i. Solid lines represent material flows, and dashed lines indicate information flows which can be demand information or production authorizations. This can be done by using either card-based system or computer-based system.

The Kanban is a simple control mechanism that depends only on one parameter per workstation: the number of kanbans at workstation i, k_i, $i = 1,\ldots, \mathcal{N} - 1$, where $\mathcal{N}$ is the total number of workstations in the system. These parameters influence both the transfer of finished parts downstream through the line and the transfer of demands upstream through the line. Let $|q|$ be the number of items in queue q. The invariant of Kanban mechanism of each workstation can be expressed as follow.

$$|K_i| + |p_i| + |b_i| = k_i, \quad i = 1, \ldots, \mathcal{N} - 1 \tag{3.1}$$

where, K_i is the station i kanban queue containing station i available kanbans, p_i the manufacturing/assembly process of station i, b_i the output buffer of station i, and k_i the total number of kanbans at station i.

This implies that the total amount of WIP in workstation i is bounded by k_i.

3.3 Other Pull Systems

3.3.1 CONWIP

CONstant Work-In-Process (CONWIP) control policy proposed by Spearman et al. (1990) maintains a constant work in process inventory in the entire production line. In the simplest implementation of a CONWIP mechanism, a new job is not started in a line until an existing job exits the line and jobs are pushed along the line in FCFS (first-come, first-serve) sequence. CONWIP system sets a WIP limit for the entire system which is equal to the total number of cards circulating within the system. When the preset WIP level is reached, no new jobs are authorized to release into the system before some job leaves when a demand occurs. A CONWIP line can be seen as a single-workstation Kanban encompassing all stations.

Figure 3.2 shows the AID of a CONWIP control policy having four workstations in series. Even though there are four workstations, the release of parts into the system is controlled only at the first workstation, and the intermediate workstations plays no control action. It is indeed considered as a single-workstation Kanban control. The manufacturing/assembling processes at each workstation are drawn as squares and buffers as ovals. M represents raw material buffer, and b the finished products buffer. Queue b_i is the output buffer of station i. Queue C contains CONWIP cards.

The CONWIP control is even simpler than Kanban control. It depends only on one parameter for the entire line: the total number of circulating cards, c. It influences both the transfer of finished parts downstream and the transfer of demands upstream through the line. There is no demand transfer between each workstation except the last and the first workstations.

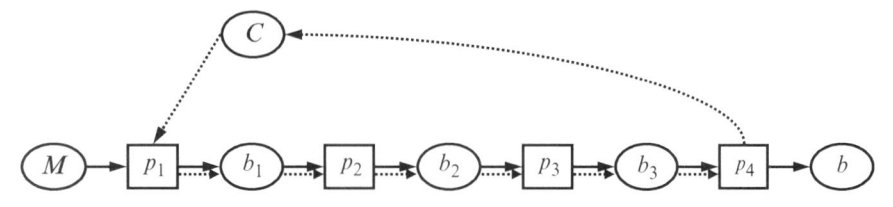

Fig. 3.2 A serial production line controlled by CONWIP

The total amount of parts in the system is bound by c and can be expressed as follow.

$$|C| + \sum |p_i| + \sum |b_i| = c, \quad i = 1, \ldots, \mathcal{N} - 1 \qquad (3.2)$$

where, C indicates the CONWIP queue containing available cards, p_i the manufacturing/assembly process of station i, b_i the output buffer of station i, and c the total number of cards in the system.

A CONWIP system behaves as follows: when a job order arrives to a CONWIP line, a card is attached to the job, provided cards are available at the beginning of the line. Otherwise, the job must wait in a backlog. When a job is processed at the final station, the card is removed and sent back to the beginning of the line, where it might be attached to the next job waiting in the backlog. No order can enter the line without its corresponding card. The primary difference between CONWIP and Kanban systems is that CONWIP pulls a job into the beginning of the line and the job goes with a kanban between workstations, while Kanban pulls jobs between all stations (Hopp and Spearman 2008).

3.3.2 Base-Stock

Base-stock control policy limits the amount of inventory between each workstation and the demand process. It tries to maintain a certain amount of WIP in each workstation. This amount is called the *basestock level* of each workstation. In other words, the basestock level of a workstation determines the maximum planned inventory of the outputs of the workstation (Lee and Zipkin 1992). To operate a Base-stock, it is necessary to transmit demand information to all workstations as demand occurs.

Figure 3.3 shows the AID of a serial production line with four workstations in series controlled by the Base-stock control policy. The manufacturing/assembling processes at each workstation are drawn as squares and buffers as ovals. M represents raw material buffer, and b the finished products buffer. Queue b_i is the output buffer of station i, and queue C_i contains the free kanbans of stage i.

Base-stock is a control mechanism that depends only on one parameter per workstation: s_i, $i = 1, \ldots, \mathcal{N} - 1$. This control mechanism does not impose limits on the individual buffer levels. This is useful in recovery from failures: when a

3.3 Other Pull Systems

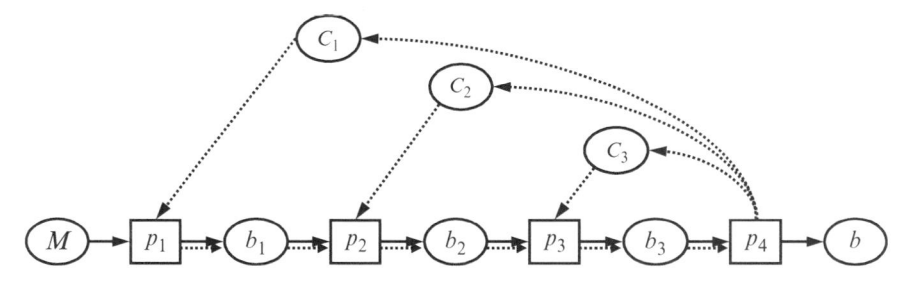

Fig. 3.3 A serial production line controlled by Base-stock

machine fails, the demand process continues to remove materials form the finished products inventory, and the machines downstream of the failure operate normally until they become starved of parts to process. The machines upstream of the failed machine receive direct demand information and operate and release parts as usual. There is therefore a build-up of inventory in front of the failed machine until it is repaired.

In Base-stock control system with $\mathcal{N}$ workstations, we have the following.

$$|C_i| + |p_i| + |b_i| = s_i - s_{i+1} + |C_{i+1}|, \quad i = 1, \ldots, \mathcal{N} - 1 \qquad (3.3)$$

$$|b_i| \leq s_i, \quad i = 1, \ldots, \mathcal{N} - 1 \qquad (3.4)$$

Inequality (3.4) shows the bound on the output buffers.

3.3.3 Hybrid Kanban-CONWIP

It is not hard to visualize combinations of the control systems just described. For example, we can imagine a system controlled by the CONWIP policy acting as a release control combined with finite buffers between workstations limiting WIP build-ups. This is a CONWIP-Kanban hybrid control policy. Under this control policy, demand information is distributed directly from the finished products buffer to authorize the production in the first workstation via CONWIP control and there also are inventory limits in each workstation as in Kanban control.

Figure 3.4 shows the AID of a serial production line with four workstations controlled by CONWIP-Kanban hybrid control policy. Queue b_i is the output buffer of stage i containing finished parts, stage-i kanbans and CONWIP cards. Queue K_i contains stage-i kanbans and queue C contains CONWIP cards. No separate kanban is needed for the synchronization of the last production stage with the production line, since the amount of material in the entire line can never exceed the inventory allowed in this buffer.

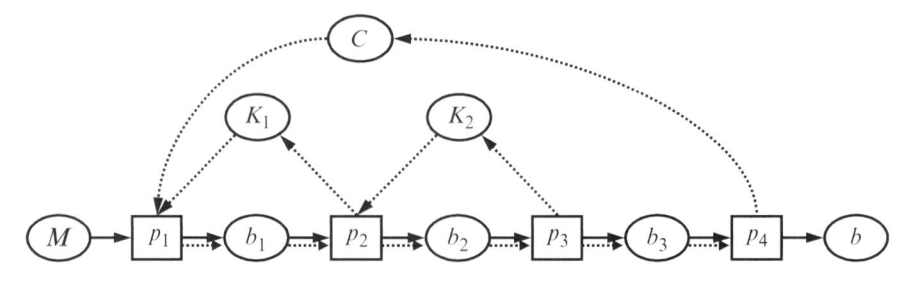

Fig. 3.4 A serial production line controlled by CONWIP-Kanban hybrid

When either a kanban card/signal or a CONWIP card/signal arrives at queue K_1 for kanban or queue C for CONWIP, it needs to wait for the other card/signal in order to release the raw material into the first station.

For more on the hybrid Kanban-CONWIP system, see Lödding (2013) and Huang et al. (2013).

We can also imagine other hybrids, such as Base-stock and Kanban, which corresponds to the Extended Kanban control developed by Dallery and Liberopoulos (2000). Another one is the Generalized Kanban control introduced by Buzacott (1989). Detail description of these control policies can be found in the respective original references.

References

Buzacott, J. A. (1989). Queuing models of kanban and MRP controlled production systems. *Engineering Cost and Production Economics, 17*, 3–20.
Dallery, Y., & Liberopoulos, G. (2000). Extended kanban control system: Combining kanban and base stock. *IIE Transactions, 32*, 369–386.
Gstettner, S., & Kuhn, H. (1996). Analysis of production control systems kanban and CONWIP. *International Journal of Production Research, 34*(11), 3253–3274.
Hopp, W. J., & Spearman, M. L. (2008). *Factory physics* (3rd ed.). New York: McGraw-Hill.
Huang, Y., Kuriger, G., & Chen, F. F. (2013). Simulation studies of hybrid pull systems of kanban and conwip in an assembly line. In A. Azevedo (Ed.), *Advances in sustainable and competitive manufacturing systems*. Cham: Springer International Publishing.
Lee, Y.-J., & Zipkin, P. (1992). Tandem queues with planned inventories. *Operations Research, 40*(5), 936–947.
Lödding, H. (2013). Hybrid Kanban/CONWIP control. In H. Lödding (Ed.), *Handbook of manufacturing control*. Berlin/Heidelberg: Springer.
Muckstadt, J. A., & Tayur, S. R. (1995). A comparison of alternative kanban control mechanisms: I, background and structural results. *IIE Transactions, 27*(1), 140–150.
Sato, R., & Praehofer, H. (1997). A discrete event model of business system – A systems theoretic foundation for information systems analysis: Part 1. *IEEE Transactions on Systems, Man, and Cybernetics, 27*(1), 1–10.
Spearman, M. L., Woodruff, D. L., & Hopp, W. J. (1990). CONWIP: A pull alternative to Kanban. *International Journal of Production Research, 23*, 879–894.

A Framework for Production Control Systems

In this book, the framework proposed by Sato and Khojasteh-Ghamari (2012) is used for comparing pull production control systems. It is based on the theory of token transaction systems. This chapter aims to describe the framework and to briefly introduce the fundamental of the theory of token transactions systems.

4.1 Token Transactions Systems

Consider a specific type of business transaction system, where queues are FIFO (first-in, first-out) types to store objects called *tokens* and every queue can have at most one input and output arrow. This system is called a *token transaction system* (Sato and Praehofer (1997) and Sato and Khojasteh-Ghamari (2012)). In a token transaction system, tokens represent parts, products, workers, or data. The AID of a token transaction system for a simple assembly process is depicted in Fig. 4.1, where activities and queues are represented by squares and ovals, respectively. It shows a serial production line governed by CONWIP. The purchased material M is processed by processes p_1 through p_4 to be a product which is stored in the place b. The output buffer of process p_i ($i = 1, 2, 3, 4$) is denoted by b_i, and the workers for processes are represented by tokens in $w_i (i = 1, 2, 3, 4)$. The queue C represents the storage place of cards.

A *workstation* is a collection of one or more machines or manual stations that perform (essentially) identical functions. The terms station, work center, and process center are synonymous with workstation. A *part* is a piece of raw material, a component, a subassembly, or an assembly that is worked on at the workstations in a plant. *Raw material* refers to parts purchased from outside the plant.

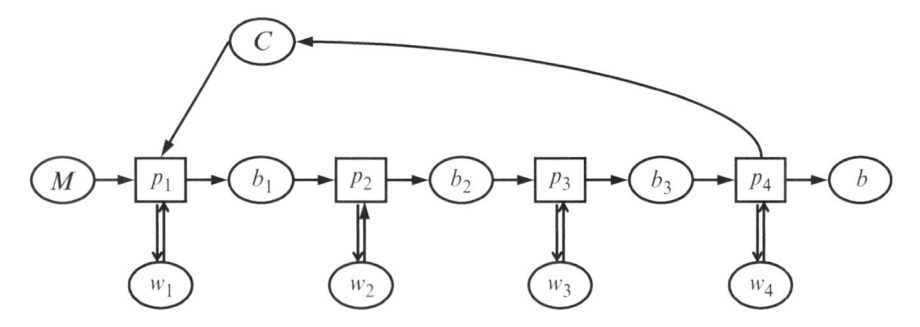

Fig. 4.1 A serial production line with four workstations controlled by CONWIP

4.1.1 Dynamics of a Token Transaction System

The time evolution of a token transaction system is defined by the state transition function, which is originally defined by the set theoretic notation by Sato and Praehofer (1997). The time evolution of the CONWIP system in Fig. 4.1 is determined by specifying the starting condition of activities and movement of tokens. We assume that there is always enough raw material in M. Then, p_1 starts its processing if more than one card exists in the card buffer C, and if the worker is available (that is, if the worker is not busy). When p_1 finishes, it outputs a token to b_1. One token in an activity, say p_1, implies that a part is being processed in the activity p_1. Also, one token in an output buffer, say, b_1, represents combination of a part and a card.

Each of the processes p_2, p_3, and p_4 will start its operation if more than one pair of part and an attached card exist in the respective input buffer, and the respective worker is available. When p_4 starts, it also outputs a card to C. As a whole, Table 4.1 will come out. In this table, "----" represents that there is no token being processed. That is, the corresponding worker is idle. "1(2)", for example, shows that one token is being processed and it will finish (be imminent) after 2 time units. As like the p_3 column, two tokens can be processed simultaneously each of which will be imminent independently.

The initial conditions in the CONWIP example shown in Table 4.1 are as follows.

- Number of tokens in C is 4.
- Each of p_1, p_2, and p_4 has one worker, but p_3 has two.
- Each activity is idle.
- The inventory in each of b_1, b_2, b_3, and b is zero.

The numbers and symbols in the first row of the state transition table depicted in Table 4.1 can be interpreted as follows. At time 373, there is no available card in the card buffer $C(C=0)$. One part is being processed at p_1 which will be imminent after 2 time units. Since a part is being processed at p_1, the corresponding worker w_2 is

4.1 Token Transactions Systems

Table 4.1 State transition table of the CONWIP

Time	C	p_1	w_1	b_1	p_2	w_2	b_2	p_3	w_3	b_3	p_4	w_4	b
373	0	1(2)	0	0	----	1	1	1(7),1(10)	0	0	1(5)	0	1
375	0	----	1	0	1(3)	0	1	1(5),1(8)	0	0	1(3)	0	1
378	0	----	1	0	----	1	2	1(2),1(5)	0	0	----	1	2
380	0	1(2)	0	0	----	1	1	1(3),1(12)	0	0	1(5)	0	2
382	0	----	1	0	1(3)	0	1	1(1),1(10)	0	0	1(3)	0	2
383	0	----	1	0	1(2)	0	0	1(9),1(12)	0	1	1(2)	0	2
385	0	1(2)	0	0	----	1	1	1(7),1(10)	0	0	1(5)	0	3

busy and is not available ($w_1 = 0$). There is no part in the first output buffer ($b_1 = 0$), and no part is being processed at p_2, and hence the respective worker is idle ($w_2 = 1$). One part is stored in buffer b_2 ($b_2 = 1$). Two parts are being processed at p_3, one will be imminent after 7 time units and the other after 10 time units. Hence, none of the respective workers is available ($w_3 = 0$). No part is in the output buffer of the third activity ($b_3 = 0$), one part is being processed in p_4 with an imminent time of 5 time units causing its worker to be busy at the moment ($w_4 = 0$). One finished product is available in the last output buffer b waiting to be delivered to the customer.

Now we explain how those numbers change in the table at the later times. In the first row, by comparing remaining times in p_1, p_3, and p_4, the most recently imminent activity (process) is p_1. When p_1 finishes at time 375 (=373 + 2), it outputs respective tokens to w_1 and b_1. Then the added tokens in b_1 allows p_2 to start at time 375, one token will move from each of b_1 and w_2 to process p_2. Since no other activities can start at 375, the state transition will grow from the time 375 to the next event.

At time 375, there are two imminent processes p_2 and p_4. Thus, the next event will be 378 (=375 + 3). The state of the system will evolve in the same way such that after a certain period of time all the numbers in a row will be repeated. This happens every 12 (=385 − 373) time units in this example.

4.1.2 Dynamic Properties of a Token Transaction System

The static structure of a token transaction system is modeled by an AID. In the AID of a token transaction system, a *path* is a series of activities and queues that follows the direction of connecting arrows among them. A path with a coincident start and end node is called a *cycle*, or a *circuit*. If a circuit contains different activities and queues (except the start and end), then it is called an *elementary circuit*. When a circuit contains a queue that gets tokens from an activity when it starts, then the activities whose outputs are the queues can be eliminated to form the shorter circuit. For example, $p_1 b_1 p_2 b_2 p_3 b_3 p_4 C p_1$ in Fig. 4.1 is a circuit and $p_1 b_1 p_2 b_2 p_3 b_3 C p_1$ is also a circuit, because C is a queue that gets a token when p_4 starts. The *cycle mean* of a circuit is defined as the sum of the holding time of the activities of the circuit, divided by the number of tokens in the circuit. The *maximum cycle mean*, λ, of an AID is the maximum value of all cycle means (Baccelli et al. 1992) and is given by

$$\lambda = \max_{\zeta} \frac{|\zeta|_h}{|\zeta|_t},$$

where, ζ ranges over the set of elementary circuits of the AID, $|\zeta|_h$ denotes the sum of the holding times of the activities in the circuit, and $|\zeta|_t$ denotes the number of tokens in the circuit. All the circuits that have maximum value of cycle mean are called *critical circuits*. A circuit consists of an activity and its workers is called an *activity circuit* (for example, $p_1 w_1 p_1$ in Fig. 4.1).

In a long-run, a token transaction system shows a periodic behavior. In Table 4.1 the period is 12 time units ($385 - 373 = 12$). That is why all the corresponding inputs of rows 373 and 385 are identical.

Now we show how to calculate the maximum cycle mean as an example. Consider the CONWIP system depicted in Fig. 4.1 in which the processing times of the four processes are set as 2, 3, 12, and 5 time units, respectively. That is, $p_1 = 2$, $p_2 = 3$, $p_3 = 12$, and $p_4 = 5$. Also, four cards are assigned to the card buffer, C. As it can be seen from the Fig. 4.1, there are five circuits where four of them are activity circuits. They are $p_1 b_1 p_2 b_2 p_3 b_3 p_4 C$, $p_1 w_1 p_1$, $p_2 w_2 p_2$, $p_3 w_3 p_3$, and $p_4 w_4 p_4$.

In the first circuit, the sum of the processing times is 22 (sum of 2, 3, 12, and 5). By observing its state transition table for a period (Table 4.1), there are 5 tokens in this circuit at any given time. For example, at time 373, one token is in each of p_1, b_2, p_4, and two tokens in p_3. Therefore, the cycle mean of this circuit will be 4.4 (=22/5). The cycle means of the remaining circuits can be calculated as shown in Table 4.2.

Notice that each of p_1, p_2 and p_4 has one worker, while the process p_3 has two. That is why the number of tokens in circuit $p_3 w_3 p_3$ is 2, but in the others is 1.

The maximum cycle mean of the system will be the largest cycle mean which is 6, making the circuit $p_3 w_3 p_3$ critical.

$$\lambda = \max\left\{\frac{22}{5}, \frac{2}{1}, \frac{3}{1}, \frac{12}{2}, \frac{5}{1}\right\} = 6.0$$

The number of commencement in a period is called the *activation frequency* of the system. The numbers of commencement and finish of an activity in a period are the same. In the period shown in Table 4.1, the activation frequency is 2 since every activity starts and ends twice within the period.

The system throughput has an inverse relation with the maximum cycle mean. Sato and Khojasteh-Ghamari (2012) proved that the maximum cycle mean, λ, of a strongly connected and live token transaction system is the reciprocal of the system throughput. That is, $TH = \lambda^{-1}$.

For more dynamic properties of token transaction systems, see Sato and Kawai (2007), and Sato and Khojasteh-Ghamari (2012).

Table 4.2 Cycle means calculation

Circuit	Sum of processing times	Number of tokens in the circuit	Cycle mean
$p_1 w_1 p_1$	2	1	$2/1 = 2$
$p_2 w_2 p_2$	3	1	$3/1 = 3$
$p_3 w_3 p_3$	12	2	$12/2 = 6$
$p_4 w_4 p_4$	5	1	$5/1 = 5$

4.2 Performance Measures

Two performance measures are used for comparing pull production control systems. They are the *average WIP* and the *system throughput*. Hereafter, we simply write "*WIP*" and "*TH*" to mean the average WIP and the system throughput, respectively. We call the sum of WIPs in a pull control system *the system WIP*. The system WIP will be the sum of the tokens located in all queues and activities in the system. The system throughput is defined as the average number of finished products produced per time unit.

The best performance for a production process can be achieved by choosing an appropriate number of cards in a pull production control system. A system has the best performance when it attains the maximum possible throughput with a minimum number of WIP. This is called the *best-case performance* by Hopp and Spearman (2008).

4.3 Application of the Framework in Comparing Control Systems

In the following two chapters, by applying the theory of token transaction systems and the framework described, we will analyze and compare the three control systems, Kanban, CONWIP, and Base-stock in two different production processes. One type is serial production lines which will be discussed in Chap. 5, and the other one is assembly types, which will be presented in Chap. 6.

References

Baccelli, F. L., Cohen, G., Olsder, G. J., & Quadrat, J. P. (1992). *Synchronization and linearity – An algebra for discrete event systems*. Chichester/New York: Wiley.

Hopp, W. J., & Spearman, M. L. (2008). *Factory physics* (3rd ed.). New York: McGraw-Hill.

Sato, R., & Kawai, A. (2007) *Organizing a business process that realizes required throughput: The principle and an application to information systems for SCM* (Discussion Paper Series No.1184). Department of Social Systems and Management, University of Tsukuba.

Sato, R., & Khojasteh-Ghamari, Y. (2012). An integrated framework for card-based production control systems. *Journal of Intelligent Manufacturing, 23*(3), 717–731.

Sato, R., & Praehofer, H. (1997). A discrete event model of business system – A systems theoretic foundation for information systems analysis: Part 1. *IEEE Transactions on Systems, Man, and Cybernetics, 27*(1), 1–10.

Analysis of Control Systems in Serial Production Lines

5

In this chapter, three pull production control systems, Kanban, CONWIP, and Base-stock are analyzed in serial production lines using the theory of token transaction systems. We provide an analytical comparison among those three control systems in a serial production line having two or more workstations, followed by a set of numerical experiments.

5.1 Comparison of Kanban and CONWIP

Using analytical queuing network models, Gstettner and Kuhn (1996) provided a quantitative comparison between Kanban and CONWIP with respect to WIP and throughput in a serial production line including six workstations with exponentially distributed processing times. Contrary to the comparative conclusions in the literature, they showed that Kanban can achieve a given production rate with a less average WIP level than CONWIP, if the card distribution in the Kanban is chosen appropriately. They defined the average number of finished parts in the output buffers as the average WIP. In the following, we analyze Kanban and CONWIP, and compare their performance in serial production lines.

Figure 4.1 in Chap. 4 showed the AID of a serial production line having four workstations controlled by CONWIP. That production process is composed of four processes p_1 to p_4 with respective workers of w_1 to w_4, where each process has output b_i ($i = 1, 2, 3$) or b.[1] The corresponding Kanban process for the same serial production line is depicted in Fig. 5.1. The first process p_1 starts when more than one token is available in each of its inputs, w_1 and K_1, where K_i is the cards buffer of the workstation i. When p_1 finishes its operation, a token will be added into each of its outputs b_1 and w_1. The process p_2 starts when more than one token is available in

---

Part of this chapter is adapted from Khojasteh and Sato (2015).

[1] See Chap. 4 for more details.

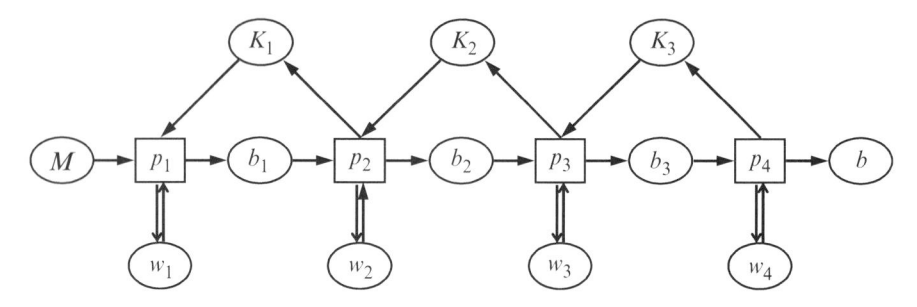

Fig. 5.1 A serial production line with four workstations controlled by Kanban

each of its inputs w_2, K_2 and b_1. Once it starts, one token is produced in each of K_1 and p_2, and when it finishes, one token is added into each of its outputs b_2 and w_2. The processes p_3 and p_4 work similarly.

In the following, we show an example of a serial production line controlled by Kanban and CONWIP with respective state transition tables.

Example 5.1 Consider a serial production line including four workstations with the CONWIP and Kanban as depicted in Figs. 4.1 and 5.1, respectively. Processing times of p_1, p_2, p_3 and p_4 are set at 2, 3, 12, and 5 time units, respectively. The process p_3 has two workers, while each of the others has only one worker. Also, initial inventory for every part is set to zero. We assume that enough raw material M is always available. Cases 5.1_KAN and 5.1_CON below show the periodic behavior of the Kanban and CONWIP, respectively.

Case **5.1_KAN**: Table 5.1 gives the state transition table for the production process with the Kanban depicted in Fig. 5.1. The number of cards are set as $k_1 = k_2 = 1$ and $k_3 = 2$, where k_i is the number of kanbans at workstation i. The system shows a periodic behavior every 12 time units. The activation frequency is 2, i.e., each activity starts twice in a period. The circuits $p_3 w_3 p_3$ and $p_3 b_3 K_3$ are critical with maximum cycle mean $\lambda = 6$ (Below, we will show how to calculate λ for this case.). The throughput is 2/12 (parts per time unit), and the system WIP is equal to 6.17.[2] It can be verified that the amount of system WIP is minimum to attain the throughput 2/12.

Case **5.1_CON**: The state transition table for the same production process under CONWIP control has been given in Table 4.1. Four cards are assigned into the system, which is the minimum number of cards to attain the maximum possible throughput. The system shows a periodic behavior every 12 time units. The activity circuit $p_3 w_3 p_3$ is critical with $\lambda = 6$. The activation frequency is 2, i.e., each activity starts twice in a period. The throughput is 2/12, and the system WIP is equal to 6.17, which is the minimum value to attain the throughput.

---

[2] Later, we will show how to calculate this system WIP.

5.1 Comparison of Kanban and CONWIP

Table 5.1 State transition of case 5.1_KAN for a period

time	K_1	p_1	w_1	b_1	K_2	p_2	w_2	b_2	K_3	p_3	w_3	b_3	p_4	w_4	b
351	0	1(2)	0	0	0	1(3)	0	0	0	1(7), 1(12)	0	0	1(5)	0	1
353	0	---	1	1	0	1(1)	0	0	0	1(5), 1(10)	0	0	1(3)	0	1
354	0	---	1	1	0	---	1	1	0	1(4), 1(9)	0	0	1(2)	0	1
356	0	---	1	1	0	---	1	1	0	1(2), 1(7)	0	0	---	1	2
358	0	1(2)	0	0	0	1(3)	0	0	0	1(12), 1(5)	0	0	1(5)	0	2
360	0	---	1	1	0	1(1)	0	0	0	1(10), 1(3)	0	0	1(3)	0	2
361	0	---	1	1	0	---	1	1	0	1(9), 1(2)	0	0	1(2)	0	2
363	0	1(2)	0	0	0	1(3)	0	0	0	1(7), 1(12)	0	0	1(5)	0	3

Table 5.2 Cycle means of the remaining circuits

Circuit	Sum of processing times	Number of tokens in the circuit	Cycle mean
$p_2 b_2 K_2$	3	1	$3/1 = 3$
$p_3 b_3 K_3$	12	2	$12/2 = 6$
$p_1 w_1 p_1$	2	1	$2/1 = 2$
$p_2 w_2 p_2$	3	1	$3/1 = 3$
$p_3 w_3 p_3$	12	2	$12/2 = 6$
$p_4 w_4 p_4$	5	1	$5/1 = 5$

To calculate the maximum cycle mean for the case 5.1_KAN in Example 5.1, we consider the Kanban system depicted in Fig. 5.1 where the processing times of the four processes have been set at 2, 3, 12, and 5 time units, respectively. That is, $p_1 = 2$, $p_2 = 3$, $p_3 = 12$, and $p_4 = 5$. As it can be seen from the figure, there are in total seven circuits of which four are activity circuits. They are $p_1 b_1 K_1$, $p_2 b_2 K_2$, $p_3 b_3 K_3$, $p_1 w_1 p_1$, $p_2 w_2 p_2$, $p_3 w_3 p_3$, and $p_4 w_4 p_4$.

In the first circuit, the sum of the processing times (which is for only one process p_1) is 2. By observing the state transition table for a period given in Table 5.1, there is only one token in this circuit at any given time. For example, at times 351 and 358, the token is in p_1, but at the remaining times it is in the output buffer b_1. Therefore, the cycle mean[3] of this circuit will be 2 ($= 2/1$). The cycle means of the remaining circuits are calculated as shown in Table 5.2.

The maximum cycle mean of the system is the largest cycle mean which is 6. It is for the two critical circuits $p_3 w_3 p_3$ and $p_3 b_3 K_3$.

$$\lambda = \max\{2, 3, 6, 2, 3, 6, 5\} = 6.0$$

Now, we show how to calculate the system WIP by using the state transition table in case 5.1_KAN. Consider its state transition table given in Table 5.1. By observing the table for a period, at time 351, five tokens (all of them are being processed at p_1 through p_4) remain in the system for 2 time unit ($353 - 351 = 2$). At the next event time (i.e. 353), six tokens remain in the system, but for 1 time unit ($354 - 353 = 1$). Similarly, 7, 7, 5, 6, and 7 tokens remain in the system for the next 2, 2, 2, 1, and 2 time units, respectively. This yields $(2 \times 5) + (1 \times 6) + (2 \times 7) + (2 \times 7) + (2 \times 5) + (1 \times 6) + (2 \times 7) = 74$ [tokens × time units] as the total holding and waiting times for a period. Since the period is 12 time units, the system WIP is 6.17 ($=74/12$) tokens.

In both cases, 5.1_KAN and 5.1_CON, the optimum system WIPs to attain the same level of throughput are the same. In the following, it is proved that this statement holds true when the same total number of cards is employed in both the systems.

---

[3] As defined in Chap. 4, the cycle mean of a circuit is the ratio of the sum of the processing times of the processes on the circuit divided by the number of tokens in the circuit.

5.1.1 Analytical Comparison

Proposition 5.1 (Khojasteh-Ghamari and Sato, 2011) Consider a serial production line with n workstations controlled by Kanban and CONWIP as depicted in Figs. 5.2 and 5.3, respectively. Assume that both the systems have the same number of workers for respective processes, the same activation frequency, and the same throughput. Let K and N be the total number of cards in the Kanban and CONWIP, respectively. Then, we have the following.

(i) $W_C < W_K$ if and only if $N < K$,
(ii) $W_C = W_K$ if and only if $N = K$,

where W_K and W_C are the average system WIP for the Kanban and CONWIP, respectively.

Proof[4] (1) Let the throughput be TH, the activation frequency ρ, and the period L. Then, we have $TH=\rho/L$, since every activity starts and ends ρ times in the period, and one token moves at every commencement (or, completion). Thus, both systems have the same period, L.

(2) Let $\overline{C}$ be a circuit. Tokens are held in activities or connecting queues. We denote $a \in A(\overline{C})$ to show that an activity a is on $\overline{C}$, and $q \in Q(\overline{C})$ if a connecting queue q is on

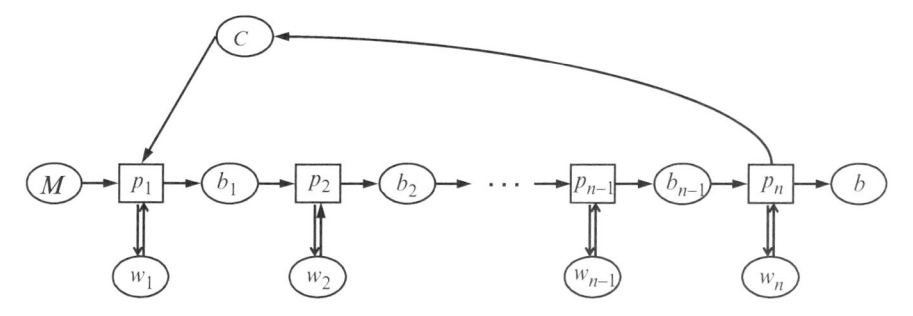

Fig. 5.2 A serial production line with n workstations controlled by CONWIP

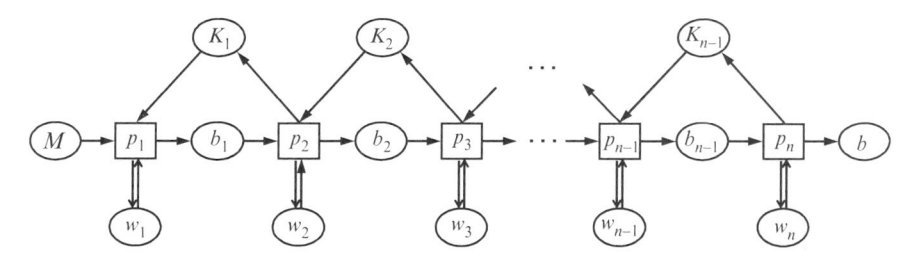

Fig. 5.3 A serial production line with n workstations controlled by Kanban

---
[4] Khojasteh-Ghamari and Sato, 2011

$\overline{C}$. The processing time of a is denoted by h_a. Let the outmost circuit in the CONWIP be F. That is, F is $Cp_1b_1p_2b_2\ldots p_{n-1}b_{n-1}C$ (see Fig. 5.2). In the Kanban, let G be $\{D_1, D_2, \ldots, D_{n-1}\}$, where $D_i (i = 1, 2, \ldots, n-1)$ is the circuit $K_ip_ib_iK_i$ with k_i tokens (see Fig. 5.3). Since the activation frequency in both the systems is the same, we have $\sum_{a \in A(F)} h_a = \sum_{a \in A(G)} h_a$, where $A(G)$ is defined as $\bigcup_{i=1}^{n-1} A(D_i)$.

(3) For a connecting queue q, denote the integration value of token in the queue for a period as h_q. The sum of integration value of the connecting queues on $\overline{C}$ is $\sum_{q \in Q(\overline{C})} h_q$. Thus, the average WIP in q is h_q/L. Let the number of tokens on $\overline{C}$ be denoted by n_C. Then, $n_C \cdot L = \rho(\sum_{a \in A(\overline{C})} h_a) + \sum_{q \in Q(\overline{C})} h_q$. The cycle time of $\overline{C}$ (the total time for a token on $\overline{C}$ to go round once) is given by $CT_C = \frac{n_C}{TH} = \frac{n_C \cdot L}{\rho}$. This cycle time is equal to $CT_C = \sum_{a \in A(\overline{C})} h_a + \left(\sum_{q \in Q(\overline{C})} h_q/\rho\right)$, because each activity in the process starts and ends for the same number of times ρ, and for the rest of time in a period, tokens are remained in the connecting queues. Thus, we have $n_C \cdot L = \rho(\sum_{a \in A(\overline{C})} h_a) + \sum_{q \in Q(\overline{C})} h_q$.

(4) The sum of integration values of the connecting queues on all activity circuits in the CONWIP and Kanban for a period is the same. In the CONWIP, let the integration value of a token in the worker for p_i ($i = 1, 2, \ldots, n$) be $h_{q_i}^C$. Then we have $h_{q_i}^C = w_i \cdot L - \rho \cdot h_i$, where w_i is the number of workers for p_i. Since the right-hand side is identical for the Kanban, we have $h_{q_i}^C = h_{q_i}^K$, where $h_{q_i}^K$ is the integration value of a process in the Kanban. In the following, the sum of integration values of all activity circuits for a period is denoted by w. That is,

$$w = \sum_{i=1}^n h_{q_i}^C = \sum_{i=1}^n h_{q_i}^K. \tag{5.1}$$

(5) In part (i) we first prove that if the total number of cards in the CONWIP be less than that in the Kanban, namely $N < \sum_{i=1}^{n-1} k_i$, where k_i is the number of cards assigned into workstation i, then $W_C < W_K$. Let the sum of integration values of all connecting queues in the CONWIP and Kanban for a period be W_q^C and W_q^K, respectively. Then,

$$W_q^C = \sum_{q \in Q(F)} h_q + w.$$

5.1 Comparison of Kanban and CONWIP

Applying Little's law on F yields $\sum_{q \in Q(F)} h_q = N \cdot L - \rho \left(\sum_{a \in A(F)} h_a \right)$.

Therefore,

$$W_q^C = N \cdot L - \rho \left(\sum_{a \in A(F)} h_a \right) + w. \qquad (5.2)$$

Since $N < \sum_{i=1}^{n-1} k_i$, we have

$$W_q^C < L \left(\sum_{i=1}^{n-1} k_i \right) - \rho \left(\sum_{a \in A(G)} h_a \right) + w = W_q^K.$$

Therefore,

$$W_C = \frac{\rho}{L} \left(\sum_{a \in A(F)} h_a \right) + \frac{1}{L} W_q^C < \frac{\rho}{L} \left(\sum_{a \in A(G)} h_a \right) + \frac{1}{L} W_q^K = W_K.$$

Now we show the opposite implication. Suppose that $W_C < W_K$. Then, we have $W_q^C < W_q^K$.

$$W_q^C = \sum_{q \in Q(F)} h_q + w = N \cdot L - \rho \left(\sum_{a \in A(F)} h_a \right) + w.$$

In the Kanban, the integration values of tokens in a circuit $D_i (i = 1, 2, \ldots, n-1)$ is given by $h_{q_i} = k_i L - \rho h_i$, where D_i is the circuit $K_i p_i b_i K_i$ with k_i tokens. Thus, the sum of integration values of all connecting queues in the Kanban for a period is given by

$$W_q^K = \sum_{i=1}^{n-1} h_{q_i} + w$$

$$= L \left(\sum_{i=1}^{n-1} k_i \right) - \rho \left(\sum_{a \in A(G)} h_a \right) + w. \qquad (5.3)$$

Since $W_q^C < W_q^K$, we have

$$N \cdot L - \rho \left(\sum_{a \in A(F)} h_a \right) + w < L \left(\sum_{i=1}^{n-1} k_i \right) - \rho \left(\sum_{a \in A(G)} h_a \right) + w.$$

Thus, $N < \sum_{i=1}^{n-1} k_i$.

(6) Now, let us prove part (ii). Assume that $N = K$, i.e., $N = \sum_{i=1}^{n-1} k_i$. Then,

$$W_C - W_K = \left(\frac{\rho}{L}\left(\sum_{a \in A(F)} h_a\right) + \frac{1}{L}W_q^C\right) - \left(\frac{\rho}{L}\left(\sum_{a \in A(G)} h_a\right) + \frac{1}{L}W_q^K\right)$$
$$= \frac{1}{L}\left(W_q^C - W_q^K\right).$$

$$W_q^C - W_q^K = \left(N \cdot I. - \rho\left(\sum_{a \in A(F)} h_a\right) + w\right) - \left(L\left(\sum_{i=1}^{n-1} k_i\right) - \rho\left(\sum_{a \in A(G)} h_a\right) + w\right)$$
$$= \left(N - \sum_{i=1}^{n-1} k_i\right) \cdot L = 0$$

Therefore, $W_C = W_K$ if and only if $N = K$. (Q.E.D.)

This proposition gives a complete characterization of comparison between Kanban and CONWIP in serial production lines. It resolves the complicated situation on comparison between these two control systems in serial production lines. It implies that in a serial production line, only the total number of cards decides the system performance.

In this proposition, the definition of WIP is different from that of Gstettner and Kuhn (1996). The system WIP is a factor that determines throughput. Therefore, if we focus only on the average value of the finished parts in the output buffers without considering the other parts that are being processed in the system, then that amount alone will not provide useful information.

5.2 Comparison of Base-Stock with Kanban and CONWIP

We have already explained the dynamic operation of CONWIP and Kanban using the concept of the token transaction system.[5] Now we specify the operation of Base-stock in the same production process. Figure 5.4 shows the corresponding production process controlled by Base-stock. The first process p_1 starts when more than one token is available in each of its inputs, w_1 and C_1. We again assume that enough raw material M is always available. When p_1 finishes, a token will be added into each of b_1 and w_1. The process p_2 starts when more than one token is available in each of its inputs w_2, b_1, and C_2. A token is produced in p_2 when it starts. The

---
[5] See Sects. 4.1 and 5.1 for CONWIP and Kanban, respectively.

5.2 Comparison of Base-Stock with Kanban and CONWIP

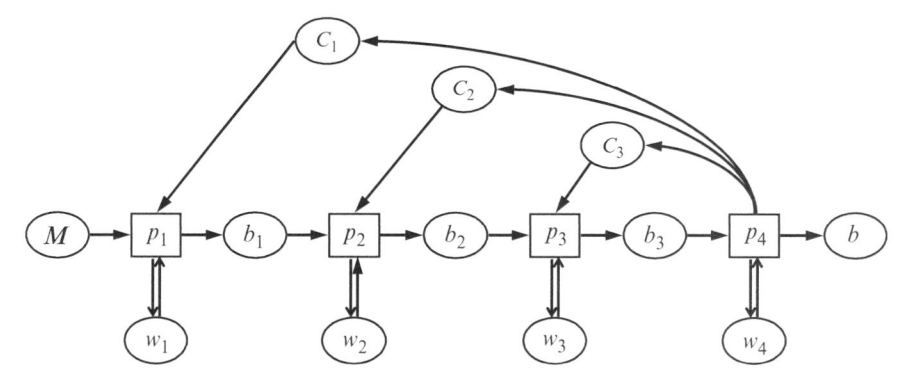

Fig. 5.4 A serial production line controlled by Base-stock

outputs of p_2 are b_2 and w_2. The process p_3 works similarly. The last process p_4 starts when more than one token is available in each of its inputs w_4 and b_3. When it starts, then a token is produced in p_4, and one token is added into each of C_1, C_2 and C_3. When it finishes, then a token is added into each of its outputs, b and w_4.

5.2.1 Comparison of Base-Stock and Kanban

The proposition below compares Base-stock and Kanban in serial production lines.

Proposition 5.2 Consider a serial production line with n workstations controlled by Kanban and Base-stock as depicted in Figs. 5.3 and 5.5, respectively. Assume that both the systems have the same number of workers for respective processes, the same activation frequency, and the same throughput. Let K and B be the total number of cards in the Kanban and Base-stock, respectively. Then, we have the following.

(i) if $B - K \leq \dfrac{1}{\lambda}\left(\sum_{i=1}^{n-2} ih_{i+1}\right)$, then $W_B \leq W_K$,

(ii) if $B = K$, then $W_B < W_K$,

where λ is the maximum cycle mean, h_i the processing time of workstation i, and W_K and W_B are the average system WIP for the Kanban and Base-stock, respectively.

Proof (1) Let the throughput be *TH*, the activation frequency ρ, and the period L. Then, for the same reason given in the proof of Proposition 5.1, both the systems have the same period L.

(2) In the Kanban, let G be $\{D_1, D_2, \ldots, D_{n-1}\}$, where $D_i (i = 1, 2, \ldots, n-1)$ is the circuit $K_i p_i b_i K_i$ with k_i tokens. In the Base-stock, let $H_i (i = 1, 2, \ldots, n-1)$ be the circuit $C_i p_i b_i p_{i+1} b_{i+1} \cdots p_{n-1} b_{n-1} C_i$, with m_i tokens (see Figs. 5.3 and 5.5).

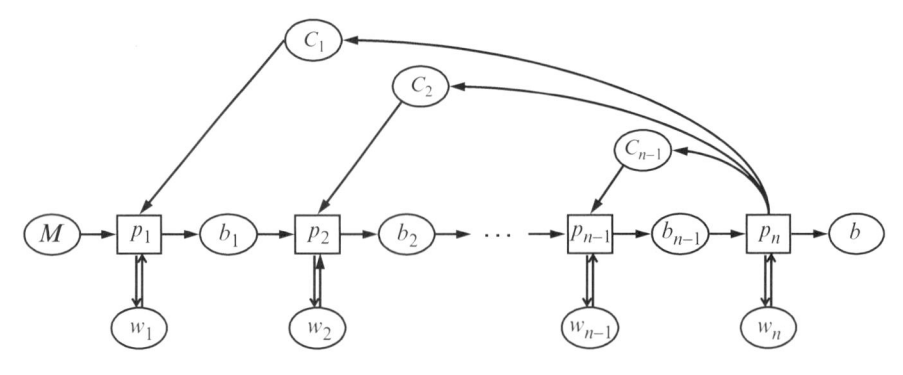

Fig. 5.5 A serial production line with n workstations controlled by Base-stock

Since the activation frequencies in both the systems are the same, we have $\sum_{a \in A(G)} h_a = \sum_{a \in A(H_1)} h_a$, where $A(G)$ is defined as $\bigcup_{i=1}^{n-1} A(D_i)$, and h_a is the processing time of the activity a.

(4) The sum of integration values of connecting queues on all activity circuits in the Kanban and Base-stock for a period is the same (for the same reason given in the proof of Proposition 5.1). That is, $w = \sum_{i=1}^{n} h_{q_i}^K = \sum_{i=1}^{n} h_{q_i}^B$, where w is the sum of integration values of all activity circuits for a period, and $h_{q_i}^K$ and $h_{q_i}^B$ are the integration value of the process i in the Kanban and Base-stock, respectively.

(5) In the Kanban, the integration value of tokens in a circuit D_i ($i = 1, 2, \ldots, n-1$) is given by $h_{q_i} = k_i L - \rho h_i$, where D_i is the circuit $K_i p_i b_i K_i$ with k_i tokens. In the Base-stock, the integration value of tokens in circuit H_i ($i = 1, 2, \ldots, n-1$) is given by $h_{q_i} = m_i L - \rho h_i$, where H_i is the circuit $C_i p_i b_i p_{i+1} b_{i+1} \ldots p_{n-1} b_{n-1} C_i$ with m_i tokens. Let the sum of integration values of all connecting queues in the Kanban and Base-stock for a period be W_q^K and W_q^B, respectively. Then,

$$W_q^K = \sum_{i=1}^{n-1} \sum_{q \in Q(D_i)} h_q + w$$

$$= \left[k_1 L - \rho \left(\sum_{a \in A(D_1)} h_a \right) \right] + \left[k_2 L - \rho \left(\sum_{a \in A(D_2)} h_a \right) \right] + \ldots + \left[k_{n-1} L - \rho \left(\sum_{a \in A(D_{n-1})} h_a \right) \right] + w \quad (5.4)$$

$$= L \left(\sum_{i=1}^{n-1} k_i \right) - \rho (h_1 + h_2 + \ldots + h_{n-1}) + w.$$

5.2 Comparison of Base-Stock with Kanban and CONWIP

And,

$$W_q^B \le \sum_{i=1}^{n-1} \sum_{q \in Q(H_i)} h_q + w \tag{5.5}$$

$$= \left[m_1 L - \rho \left(\sum_{a \in A(H_1)} h_a \right) \right] + \left[m_2 L - \rho \left(\sum_{a \in A(H_2)} h_a \right) \right] + \ldots$$

$$+ \left[m_{n-1} L - \rho \left(\sum_{a \in A(H_{n-1})} h_a \right) \right] + w$$

$$= [m_1 L - \rho(h_1 + h_2 + \ldots + h_{n-1})] + [m_2 L - \rho(h_2 + \ldots + h_{n-1})] + \ldots$$
$$+ [m_{n-1} L - \rho(h_{n-1})] + w$$

$$= L \left(\sum_{i=1}^{n-1} m_i \right) - \rho(h_1 + 2h_2 + \ldots + (n-1)h_{n-1}) + w \tag{5.6}$$

Note that the inequality used in (5.5) is because of the existence of some common activities and connecting queues among the elementary circuits[6] in the Base-stock. Now, subtracting W_q^K in (5.4) from both the sides of (5.6) yields

$$W_q^B - W_q^K \le (B - K)L - \rho(h_2 + 2h_3 + \ldots + (n-2)h_{n-1}), \tag{5.7}$$

where $K = \sum_{i=1}^{n-1} k_i$, and $B = \sum_{i=1}^{n-1} m_i$.

If $B - K \le \dfrac{h_2 + 2h_3 + \ldots + (n-2)h_{n-1}}{\lambda}$, then

$(B - K)L - \rho(h_2 + 2h_3 + \ldots + (n-2)h_{n-1}) \le 0$. By (5.7),

$$W_q^B - W_q^K \le (B - K)L - \rho(h_2 + 2h_3 + \ldots + (n-2)h_{n-1}) \le 0, \quad \text{or} \quad W_q^B \le W_q^K. \text{ Therefore,}$$

$$W_B = \frac{\rho}{L} \left(\sum_{a \in A(H_1)} h_a \right) + \frac{1}{L} W_q^B \le \frac{\rho}{L} \left(\sum_{a \in A(G)} h_a \right) + \frac{1}{L} W_q^K = W_K.$$

Thus, $W_B \le W_K$. This concludes the proof of part (i).

---

[6] If a circuit contains different activities and queues (except the start and end), then it is called an elementary circuit.

6) Now, let us prove part (ii). Assume that $B = K$. Then, in (5.7),

$$W_q^K - W_q^B \geq \rho(h_2 + 2h_3 + \ldots + (n-2)h_{n-1}) > 0, \quad \text{or} \quad W_q^B < W_q^K.$$ Thus, $W_B < W_K$. (Q.E.D.)

The statement (i) in this proposition implies that if the optimum number of cards in both the control systems satisfies the condition, which does not depend on the processing time of the first station (h_1), then $W_B \leq W_K$. In fact, the right hand side is decided by the structure of the process. Once it is given, the whole performance is decided only by the number of cards, B and K.

Contrary to the case of Kanban and CONWIP, the comparison between Kanban and Base-stock cannot be completely characterized. The statements in this proposition are not in "if and only if" form, but they are best possible forms. In other words, this proposition is one of the best possible forms in the sense that the respective converses do not hold true. It suffices to show that there exists at least an example for the converse. The following example shows that each converse implications of (i) and (ii) in Proposition 5.2 does not hold.[7]

Example 5.2 Consider a serial production line including four workstations with the Kanban and Base-stock as depicted in Figs. 5.1 and 5.4, respectively. Processing times of p_1, p_2, p_3 and p_4 are set at 5, 12, 10, and 7 time units, respectively. That is, $h_1 = 5$, $h_2 = 12$, $h_3 = 10$ and $h_4 = 7$. The process p_2 has two workers, while each of the others has only one worker. Also, initial inventory for every part is set to zero. We assume that enough raw material M is always available. Cases 5.2_BAS and 5.2_KAN below show the periodic behavior of the Base-stock and Kanban, respectively.

Case **5.2_BAS:** Table 5.3 shows the state transition table for the production process with the Base-stock. The number of cards are set as $m_1 = 4$, $m_2 = 3$ and $m_3 = 2$, (namely, $B = 9$) which are the minimum number of cards to attain the maximum possible throughput. The system shows a periodic behavior every 10 time units. Activity circuit $p_3w_3p_3$ is critical with maximum cycle mean $\lambda = 10$. $\rho = 1$, i.e., each activity starts once in a period. The throughput is 1/10, and the system WIP is equal to 5.90. That is, $W_B = 5.90$. It can be verified that the value of system WIP is minimum to attain the throughput $0.10 (= 1/10)$.

Case **5.2_KAN:** Table 5.4 gives the state transition table for the same production process with the Kanban. The number of kanbans are set as $k_1 = k_3 = 1$ and $k_2 = 2$, that is $K = 4$. The system shows a periodic behavior every 10 time units. Circuit $p_3w_3p_3$ is critical with $\lambda = 10$, and $\rho = 1$. The throughput is $0.10 (= 1/10)$, and the system WIP is equal to 6.30 ($W_K = 6.30$), which is the minimum value to attain the throughput.

Here we show again how to calculate the system WIP in case 5.2_KAN by using the state transition table. Consider Table 5.4. By observing the state transition table

---

[7] Assumptions and parameters considered in Examples 5.2, 5.3, and 5.4 are given in Table 5.10.

5.2 Comparison of Base-Stock with Kanban and CONWIP

Table 5.3 State transition of 5.2_BAS for a period

Time	C_1	p_1	w_1	b_1	C_2	p_2	w_2	b_2	C_3	p_3	w_3	b_3	p_4	w_4	b
535	0	1(3)	0	0	0	---, 1(10)	1	1	1	1(1)	0	0	---	1	1
536	0	1(2)	0	0	0	---, 1(9)	1	0	0	1(10)	0	0	1(7)	0	1
538	0	---	1	1	0	---, 1(7)	1	0	0	1(8)	0	0	1(5)	0	1
543	0	1(5)	0	0	0	1(12),1(2)	0	0	1	1(3)	0	0	---	1	2
545	0	1(3)	0	0	0	1(10), ---	1	1	1	1(1)	0	0	---	1	2

50   5 Analysis of Control Systems in Serial Production Lines

Table 5.4 State transition of 5.2_KAN for a period

Time	K_1	p_1	w_1	b_1	K_2	p_2	w'_2	b_2	K_3	p_3	w'_3	b_3	p_4	w_4	b
524	0	1(5)	0	0	0	1(2),1(12)	0	0	0	1(10)	0	0	1(7)	0	1
526	0	1(3)	0	0	0	---,1(10)	1	1	0	1(8)	0	0	1(5)	0	1
529	0	---	1	1	0	---,1(7)	1	1	0	1(5)	0	0	1(2)	0	1
531	0	---	1	1	0	---,1(5)	1	1	0	1(3)	0	0	---	1	2
534	0	1(5)	0	0	0	1(12),1(2)	0	0	0	1(10)	0	0	1(7)	0	2

5.2 Comparison of Base-Stock with Kanban and CONWIP

for a period, at time 524, five tokens (all of them are being processed at p_1 through p_4) remain in the system for 2 time unit (526 − 524 = 2). At the next event time (i.e. 526), six tokens remain in the system, but for 3 time unit (529 − 526 = 3). Similarly, 7 tokens remain in the system for the next 2 and 3 time units. This yields $(2 \times 5) + (3 \times 6) + (2 \times 7) + (3 \times 7) = 63$ [tokens x time unit] as the total holding and waiting times for a period. Since the period is 10 time units, the system WIP is 63/10 tokens. That is, $W_K = 6.30$.

Cases 5.2_BAS and 5.2_KAN show that each converse implications of (i) and (ii) in Proposition 5.2 does not hold. Because it can be simply verified that $W_B < W_K$, however, $B \neq K$, and $B - K = 9 - 4 > \frac{h_2 + 2h_3}{\lambda} = \frac{12 + 2(10)}{10}$, in the same notation of Proposition 5.2.

5.2.2 Comparison of Base-stock and CONWIP

The following proposition compares Base-stock and CONWIP in serial production lines.

Proposition 5.3 Consider a serial production line with n workstations controlled by CONWIP and Base-stock. Assume that both the systems have the same workers for respective processes, the same activation frequency, and the same throughput. Let N and B be the total number of cards in the CONWIP and Base-stock, respectively. Then, we have the following.

(i) if $B - N \leq \frac{1}{\lambda}\left(\sum_{i=1}^{n-2} i h_{i+1}\right)$, then $W_B \leq W_C$,

(ii) if $B = N$, then $W_B < W_C$,

where λ is the maximum cycle mean, h_i the processing time of workstation i, and W_C and W_B are the average system WIP for the CONWIP and Base-stock, respectively.

Proof (1) Let the throughput be TH, the activation frequency ρ, and the period L. Then, for the same reason given in the proof of Proposition 5.1, both the systems have the same period L.

Let the outmost circuit in the CONWIP be F. That is, F is $Cp_1 b_1 p_2 b_2 \ldots p_{n-1} b_{n-1} C$ (see Fig. 5.2). In the Base-stock, let $H_i (i = 1, 2, \ldots, n-1)$ be the circuit $C_i p_i b_i p_{i+1} b_{i+1} \ldots p_{n-1} b_{n-1} C_i$, with m_i tokens (see Fig. 5.5). Since the activation frequencies in both the systems are the same, we have $\sum_{a \in A(F)} h_a = \sum_{a \in A(H_1)} h_a$, where h_a is the processing time of the activity a.

(2) For the same reason given in the proof of Proposition 5.1, the sum of integration values of connecting queues on all activity circuits for a period in both the CONWIP and Base-stock is the same. That is, $w = \sum_{i=1}^{n} h_{q_i}^C = \sum_{i=1}^{n} h_{q_i}^B$, where w is the sum of integration values of all activity circuits for a period, and $h_{q_i}^C$ and $h_{q_i}^B$ are the integration value of the process i in the CONWIP and Base-stock, respectively.

(3) Now we prove part (i). Let the sum of integration values of all connecting queues in the CONWIP and Base-stock for a period be W_q^C and W_q^B, respectively. Then, as we showed in the proof of Proposition 5.1,

$W_q^C = \sum_{q \in Q(F)} h_q + w$. For circuit F, we have $\sum_{q \in O(F)} h_q = N \cdot L - \rho \left(\sum_{a \in A(F)} h_a \right)$,

where N is the total number of cards in the CONWIP. Therefore,

$$W_q^C = N \cdot L - \rho \left(\sum_{a \in A(F)} h_a \right) + w \qquad (5.8)$$
$$= N \cdot L - \rho(h_1 + h_2 + \cdots + h_{n-1}) + w.$$

And,

$$W_q^B \leq \sum_{i=1}^{n-1} \sum_{q \in Q(H_i)} h_q + w$$
$$= \left[m_1 L - \rho \left(\sum_{a \in A(H_1)} h_a \right) \right] + \left[m_2 L - \rho \left(\sum_{a \in A(H_2)} h_a \right) \right]$$
$$+ \ldots + \left[m_{n-1} L - \rho \left(\sum_{a \in A(H_{n-1})} h_a \right) \right] + w$$
$$= [m_1 L - \rho(h_1 + h_2 + \ldots + h_{n-1})] + [m_2 L - \rho(h_2 + \ldots + h_{n-1})]$$
$$+ \ldots + [m_{n-1} L - \rho(h_{n-1})] + w$$
$$= L \left(\sum_{i=1}^{n-1} m_i \right) - \rho(h_1 + 2h_2 + \ldots + (n-1)h_{n-1}) + w. \qquad (5.9)$$

Subtracting W_q^C in (5.8) from both sides of (5.9) yields

$$W_q^B - W_q^C \leq (B - N)L - \rho(h_2 + 2h_3 + \ldots + (n-2)h_{n-1}), \qquad (5.10)$$

where, $B = \sum_{i=1}^{n-1} m_i$.

5.2 Comparison of Base-Stock with Kanban and CONWIP

If $B - N \leq \dfrac{h_2 + 2h_3 + \ldots + (n-2)h_{n-1}}{\lambda}$, then

$(B-N)L - \rho(h_2 + 2h_3 + \ldots + (n-2)h_{n-1}) \leq 0$.

By (5.10), $W_q^B - W_q^C \leq (B-N)L - \rho(h_2 + 2h_3 + \ldots + (n-2)h_{n-1}) \leq 0$, or $W_q^B \leq W_q^C$. Therefore,

$$W_B = \frac{\rho}{L}\left(\sum_{a \in A(H_1)} h_a\right) + \frac{1}{L}W_q^B \leq \frac{\rho}{L}\left(\sum_{a \in A(F)} h_a\right) + \frac{1}{L}W_q^C = W_C.$$

This concludes the proof of part (i).

(4) Now, we prove part (ii). Assume that $B = N$. Then, in (5.10), $W_q^C - W_q^B \geq \rho(h_2 + 2h_3 + \ldots + (n-2)h_{n-1}) > 0$, or $W_q^B < W_q^C$. Thus, $W_B < W_C$. (Q.E.D.)

The statement (i) in this proposition implies that if the optimum number of cards in both the control systems satisfies the condition, which does not depend on the processing time of the first station (h_1), then $W_B \leq W_C$. In fact, the right hand side is decided by the structure of the process. Once it is given, the whole performance is decided only by the number of cards, B and N.

Here again, we cannot completely characterize the comparison between Base-stock and CONWIP. The statements in this proposition are not in "if and only if" form, but they are best possible forms. We give an example that shows the converse implication of (i) does not hold true.

The following example shows that the converse implication of (i) in Proposition 5.3 does not hold.

Example 5.3 This example shows that the converse implication of (i) in Proposition 5.3 does not hold. Consider a serial production line including four workstations with the CONWIP and Base-stock as depicted in Figs. 4.1 and 5.4, respectively. Processing times of p_1, p_2, p_3 and p_4 are set at 5, 12, 3, and 2 time units, respectively. That is, $h_1 = 5$, $h_2 = 12$, $h_3 = 3$ and $h_4 = 2$. Same as the previous example, the process p_2 has two workers, while each of the others has only one worker. Also, initial inventory for every part is set to zero, and it is assumed that enough raw material M is always available. Cases 5.3_BAS and 5.3_CON below show the results for the Base-stock and CONWIP, respectively.

Case **5.3_BAS:** Table 5.5 shows the state transition table for the production process with the Base-stock. The number of cards are set as $m_1 = 4$, $m_2 = 3$ and $m_3 = 1$, which are the minimum number of cards to attain the maximum possible throughput ($B = 8$). The system shows a periodic behavior every 12 time units. Activity circuit $p_2w_2p_2$ is critical with $\lambda = 6$, and $\rho = 2$, i.e., each activity starts twice in a period. The throughput is 2/12, and the system WIP is equal to 5.67. That is $W_B = 5.67$.

Table 5.5 State transition of 5.3_BAS for a period

Time	C_1	p_1	w'_1	b_1	C_2	p_2	w'_2	b_2	C_3	p_3	w'_3	b_3	p_4	w_4	b
467	0	1(5)	0	0	0	1(7),1(12)	0	0	0	1(3)	0	0	---	1	1
470	0	1(2)	0	0	0	1(4),1(9)	0	0	0	---	1	0	1(2)	0	1
472	0	1(5)	0	1	1	1(2),1(7)	0	0	1	---	1	0	---	1	2
474	0	1(3)	0	1	0	1(12),1(5)	0	0	0	1(3)	0	0	---	1	2
477	0	---	1	1	0	1(9),1(2)	0	0	0	---	1	0	1(2)	0	2
479	0	1(5)	0	0	0	1(7),1(12)	0	0	0	1(3)	0	0	---	1	3

Table 5.6 State transition of 5.3_CON for a period

Time	C	p_1	w_1	b_1	p_2	w_2	b_2	p_3	w_3	b_3	p_4	w_4	b
425	0	1(5)	0	1	1(2),1(9)	0	0	----	1	0	1(2)	0	1
427	0	1(3)	0	0	1(12),1(7)	0	0	1(3)	0	0	----	1	2
430	0	1(5)	0	1	1(9),1(4)	0	0	----	1	0	1(2)	0	2
432	0	1(3)	0	1	1(7),1(2)	0	0	----	1	0	----	1	3
434	0	1(1)	0	0	1(5),1(12)	0	0	1(3)	0	0	----	1	3
435	0	----	1	1	1(4),1(11)	0	0	1(2)	0	0	----	1	3
437	0	1(5)	0	1	1(2),1(9)	0	0	----	1	0	1(2)	0	3

Case **5.3_CON:** The state transition table for the same production process with the CONWIP is given in Table 5.6. Four cards are assigned into the system ($N = 4$), which is the minimum number of cards to attain the maximum possible throughput. The system shows a periodic behavior every 12 time units. Circuit $p_2 w_2 p_2$ is critical with $\lambda = 6$, and $\rho = 2$. The throughput is 2/12, and the system WIP is equal to 5.67 ($W_C = 5.67$).

Case 5.3_BAS and 5.3_CON show that the converse implication of (i) in Proposition 5.3 does not hold. Because $W_B \leq W_C$, but $B - N = 8 - 4 > \frac{h_2 + 2h_3}{\lambda} = \frac{12 + 2(3)}{6}$, in the same notation of Proposition 5.3.

However, we failed to find examples for the converse of part (ii). It seems that in Proposition 5.3 with $n > 2$, when both the systems perform optimally, the if-condition of part (ii) cannot be satisfied under any circumstance. Optimality here refers to the fact that the system attains maximum possible throughput by employing the least number of cards, and hence has a minimum amount of the system WIP. As it can be seen in Figs. 5.2 and 5.5, the outmost circuits in both the systems (i.e., circuit $C p_1 b_1 p_2 b_2 \ldots p_{n-1} b_{n-1} C$ in the CONWIP, and $C_1 p_1 b_1 p_2 b_2 \ldots p_{n-1} b_{n-1} C_1$ in the Base-stock) have the same components. Therefore, in order for both the systems to attain the maximum rate of throughput with minimum amount of WIP, the same number of cards is required to assign into each of C and C_1. In fact, the number of cards assigned into C is the total number of cards in the CONWIP, denoted by N. However, the Base-stock needs more cards in the other nonactivity circuits (i.e., circuits $C_i p_i b_i p_{i+1} b_{i+1} \ldots p_{n-1} b_{n-1} C_i$, $1 < i < n$) to operate properly. Thus, $B > N$. This would be a reason that we failed to find an example to show whether the converse implication of (ii) holds true.

5.2.3 Discussions

For a serial production process in the Proposition 5.2, some Kanban and Base-stock cases, which have the same level of throughput satisfy the if-condition of (i), and then $W_B \leq W_K$ certainly holds. However, in the following, we give an example that dissatisfies the if-condition, and then $W_B > W_K$. In a similar way, in Proposition 5.3 (for CONWIP and Base-stock cases), this example shows that $W_B > W_C$, and of

Table 5.7 State transition of 5.4_BAS for a period

Time	C_1	p_1	w_1	b_1	C_2	p_2	w_2	b_2	C_3	p_3	w_3	b_3	p_4	w_4	b
808	0	1(5)	0	0	1	----, 1(7)	1	0	1	1(9)	0	0	----	1	1
813	0	----	1	0	0	1(12),1(2)	0	0	1	1(4)	0	0	----	1	1
815	0	----	1	0	0	1(10), ----	1	1	1	1(2)	0	0	----	1	1
817	0	----	1	0	0	1(8), ----	1	0	0	1(10)	0	0	1(1)	0	1
818	0	1(5)	0	0	1	1(7), ----	1	0	1	1(9)	0	0	----	1	2

5.2 Comparison of Base-Stock with Kanban and CONWIP

Table 5.8 State transition of 5.4_CON for a period

Time	C	p_1	w_1	b_1	p_2	w_2	b_2	p_3	w_3	b_3	p_4	w_4	b
797	0	1 (5)	0	0	----, 1(7)	1	0	1 (10)	0	0	1 (1)	0	1
798	0	1 (4)	0	0	----, 1(6)	1	0	1(9)	0	0	----	1	2
802	0	----	1	0	1(12),1(2)	0	0	1(5)	0	0	----	1	2
804	0	----	1	0	1(10), ----	1	1	1(3)	0	0	----	1	2
807	0	1 (5)	0	0	1(7), ----	1	0	1 (10)	0	0	1 (1)	0	2

course $B - N > \frac{1}{\lambda} \left(\sum_{i=1}^{n-2} i h_{i+1} \right)$. This implies that the Base-stock is not always superior to Kanban and CONWIP.

Example 5.4 Concerning Propositions 5.2 and 5.3, this example shows that Base-stock does not necessarily outperform Kanban and CONWIP. Consider a serial production line with four workstations as depicted in Figs. 4.1, 5.1, and 5.4 with the CONWIP, Kanban, and Base-stock, respectively. We set the processing times of p_1, p_2, p_3 and p_4 at 5, 12, 10, and 1 time units, respectively. Same as the previous examples, the process p_2 has two workers, while each of the others has only one worker. Also, initial inventory for every part is set to zero. Cases 5.4_BAS, 5.4_CON and 5.4_KAN below show the results for the Base-stock, CONWIP, and Kanban, respectively.

Case **5.4_BAS**: The state transition table for a period of the Base-stock is given in Table 5.7. The number of cards are set as $m_1 = 3, m_2 = 3$, and $m_3 = 2$ (i.e., $B = 8$), which are the minimum number of cards to attain the maximum possible throughput. The system shows a periodic behavior every 10 time units. Activity circuit $p_3 w_3 p_3$ is critical with maximum cycle mean $\lambda = 10$. The throughput is 0.10 (= 1/10), and the system WIP is equal to 6.60. That is, $W_B = 6.60$.

Case **5.4_CON**: Table 5.8 shows a part of the state transition table for the production process with the CONWIP. Three cards are assigned into the system ($N = 3$), which is the minimum number of cards to attain the maximum possible throughput. The system shows a periodic behavior every 10 time units. Circuit $p_3 w_3 p_3$ is critical with $\lambda = 10$. The throughput is 0.10 (= 1/10), and $W_C = 5.30$.

Case **5.4_KAN**: The state transition table for a period is given in Table 5.9. Initial cards are set as $k_1 = k_3 = 1$ and $k_2 = 2$, i.e., $K = 4$. Circuit $p_3 w_3 p_3$ is critical with $\lambda = 10$. Each activity starts once in a period, the period is 10 time units. The system throughput is 0.10 (= 1/10), and $W_K = 6.30$.

Table 5.9 State transition of 5.4_KAN for a period

Time	K_1	p_1	w_1	b_1	K_2	p_2	w_2	b_2	K_3	p_3	w_3	b_3	p_4	w_4	b
788	0	1(4)	0	0	0	1(1),1(11)	0	0	0	1(9)	0	0	---	1	1
789	0	1(3)	0	0	0	---, 1(10)	1	1	0	1(8)	0	0	---	1	1
792	0	---	1	1	0	---, 1(7)	1	1	0	1(5)	0	0	---	1	1
797	0	1(5)	0	0	0	1(12),1(2)	0	0	0	1(10)	0	0	1(1)	0	1
798	0	1(4)	0	0	0	1(11),1(1)	0	0	0	1(9)	0	0	---	1	2

Table 5.10 Parameters in Examples 5.2, 5.3, and 5.4

	Number of work-stations	Number of workers/ machines	Processing times	Base-stock Number of cards	Base-stock Critical circuit	λ	W_B	Kanban Number of cards	Kanban Critical circuit	λ	W_K	CONWIP Number of cards	CONWIP Critical circuit	λ	W_C
Example 5.2	4	$w_1 = 1$ $w_2 = 2$ $w_3 = 1$ $w_4 = 1$	$h_1 = 5$ $h_2 = 12$ $h_3 = 10$ $h_4 = 7$	$m_1 = 4$ $m_2 = 3$ $m_3 = 2$	$p_3w_3p_3$	10	5.90	$k_1 = 1$ $k_2 = 2$ $k_3 = 1$	$p_3w_3p_3$	10	6.30	----			
Example 5.3	4	$w_1 = 1$ $w_2 = 2$ $w_3 = 1$ $w_4 = 1$	$h_1 = 5$ $h_2 = 12$ $h_3 = 3$ $h_4 = 2$	$m_1 = 4$ $m_2 = 3$ $m_3 = 1$	$p_2w_2p_2$	6	5.67	----				$N = 4$	$p_2w_2p_2$	6	5.67
Example 5.4	4	$w_1 = 1$ $w_2 = 2$ $w_3 = 1$ $w_4 = 1$	$h_1 = 5$ $h_2 = 12$ $h_3 = 10$ $h_4 = 1$	$m_1 = 3$ $m_2 = 3$ $m_3 = 2$	$p_3w_3p_3$	10	6.60	$k_1 = 1$ $k_2 = 2$ $k_3 = 1$	$p_3w_3p_3$	10	6.30	$N = 3$	$p_3w_3p_3$	10	5.30

Comparison of the system WIPs in cases 5.4_BAS and 5.4_CON reveals the fact that Base-stock does not necessarily outperform CONWIP. Because, $W_C = 5.30 < 6.60 = W_B$. It can be easily verified that the if-condition does not hold, because $B - N = 8 - 3 > \frac{h_2 + 2h_3}{\lambda} = \frac{12 + 2(10)}{10}$.

This example also shows that Base-stock does not necessarily outperform Kanban, either. Because in cases 5.4_BAS and 5.4_KAN, one can see that $W_K < W_B$ (and of course $B - K = 8 - 4 > \frac{h_2 + 2h_3}{\lambda} = \frac{12 + 2(10)}{10}$). Therefore, the if-conditions of Propositions 5.2 and 5.3 are meaningful, and as a consequence, Base-stock is not always superior to CONWIP and Kanban. In fact, appropriate design of the whole system decides the superior one in certain situation.

5.3 Highlights of the Comparison Method

It should be noted that the comparison method of the current study to compare the control systems in serial production lines differs from that of Bonvik et al. (1997) from the following aspects.

1. They defined the WIP as only the amount of the material that has been loaded on the first machine, but has not yet been delivered to satisfy demand. In fact, they did not consider the parts that are authorized for loading at the first machine inventory until they are actually loaded. While, we define the system WIP as the average number of tokens in the system, which includes the tokens corresponding to the available kanbans (cards) as the authorized parts for loading at machines as well.
2. In their considered model, machine breakdown during a process is possible that follows an exponential distribution, while we assume that no failure occurs.
3. Concerning the Base-stock system, they set all basestock levels throughout the production line except the last, as zero. That is, each machine except the last one has a basestock level of zero. While, we assume that there is no limit on the basestock levels.

5.4 Conclusions

In this chapter, by using the theory of token transaction systems, we compared the performance of three production control systems, Kanban, CONWIP, and Base-stock in serial production lines.

In comparison of Kanban and CONWIP in serial production lines, Proposition 5.1 gives a complete characterization. That is, CONWIP is superior to Kanban, if and only if, the total number of cards in the CONWIP is less than that in the Kanban. Superiority here refers to the fact that the minimum system WIP is smaller than the other to attain the same rate of throughput. This proposition resolves the complicated situation on comparison between Kanban and CONWIP in serial production lines. It implies that in a serial production line, only the total number of cards decides the system performance.

In comparison of Base-stock with Kanban and CONWIP, the situation is complicated, so that we cannot completely characterize it. Base-stock outperforms Kanban in some cases, while it does not in other cases. This happens in the comparison with CONWIP, too. That is, Base-stock outperforms CONWIP in some cases, while it does not in other cases. We clarified that the superiority of one over another is determined by a configuration of parameters, such as processing time of activities (except the processing time of the first activity, h_1), number of workers, and number of cards employed in the line (Propositions 5.2 and 5.3). In a production line with a certain configuration, for example, Base-stock is superior to Kanban. Therefore, if a line with such a certain configuration was considered, then it could result in the superiority of Base-stock to Kanban.

References

Bonvik, A. M., Couch, C. E., & Gershwin, S. B. (1997). A comparison of production-line control mechanisms. *International Journal of Production Research, 35*(3), 789–804.

Gstettner, S., & Kuhn, H. (1996). Analysis of production control systems kanban and CONWIP. *International Journal of Production Research, 34*(11), 3253–3274.

Khojasteh-Ghamari, Y., & Sato, R. (2011). Managing an assembly production process with a proper control policy. *International Journal of Manufacturing Technology and Management, 22*(1), 2–25.

Khojasteh, Y., & Sato, R. (2015). Selection of a pull production control system in multi-stage production processes. *International Journal of Production Research, 53*(14), 4363–4379.

Analysis of Control Systems in Assembly Production Processes 6

This chapter presents performance comparisons of three pull production control systems, Kanban, CONWIP, and Base-stock, in assembly production processes. By means of the theory of token transaction systems, we provide an analytical comparison among them in assembly production processes, followed by numerical experiments. We first analyze Kanban and CONWIP and provide comparative results between them. Then, we analyze Base-stock, and present comparative results of that with Kanban.

6.1 Analysis of Kanban and CONWIP

6.1.1 A Simple Assembly Production Process

Consider an assembly production process with three stages as shown in Fig. 6.1. The finished product is assembled from two distinctive subassemblies, and each subassembly is made up of two distinctive parts. The product is assembled from one unit of each subassembly, and each of the subassemblies is fabricated by using one unit of each part. The activity interaction diagrams for this production process governed by CONWIP and Kanban are depicted in Figs. 6.2 and 6.3, respectively.

6.1.1.1 Numerical Examples

In the following, we show four examples of state transition of the assembly production processes depicted in Figs. 6.2 and 6.3. Three of them are CONWIP controls, while the other is a Kanban controlled production process. Since the number of tokens on a circuit remains the same at any state transition, we can control the WIP on a circuit by initial placement of tokens. Initial tokens on circuits

---

Part of this chapter is adapted from Khojasteh and Sato (2015).

64   6 Analysis of Control Systems in Assembly Production Processes

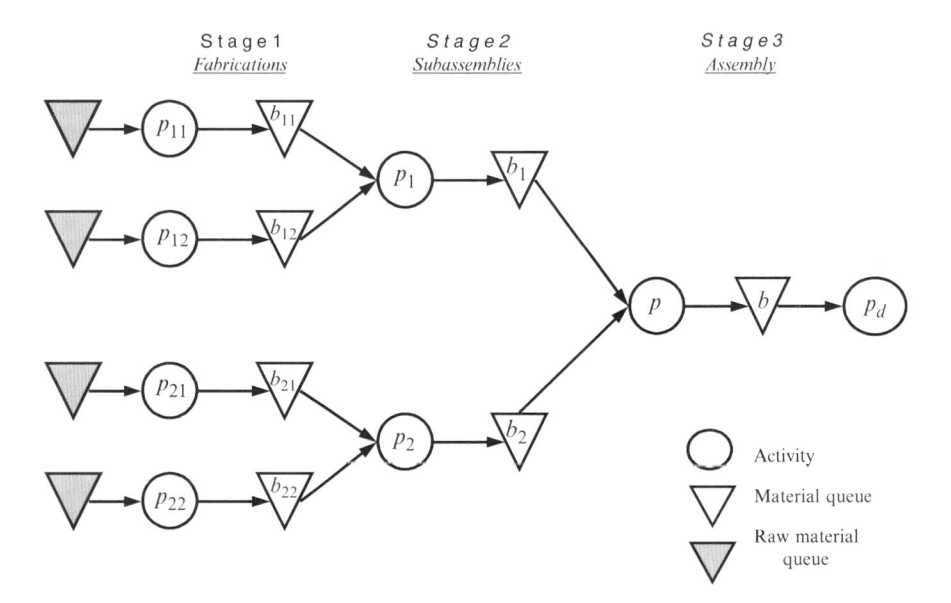

Fig. 6.1 A simple assembly production process

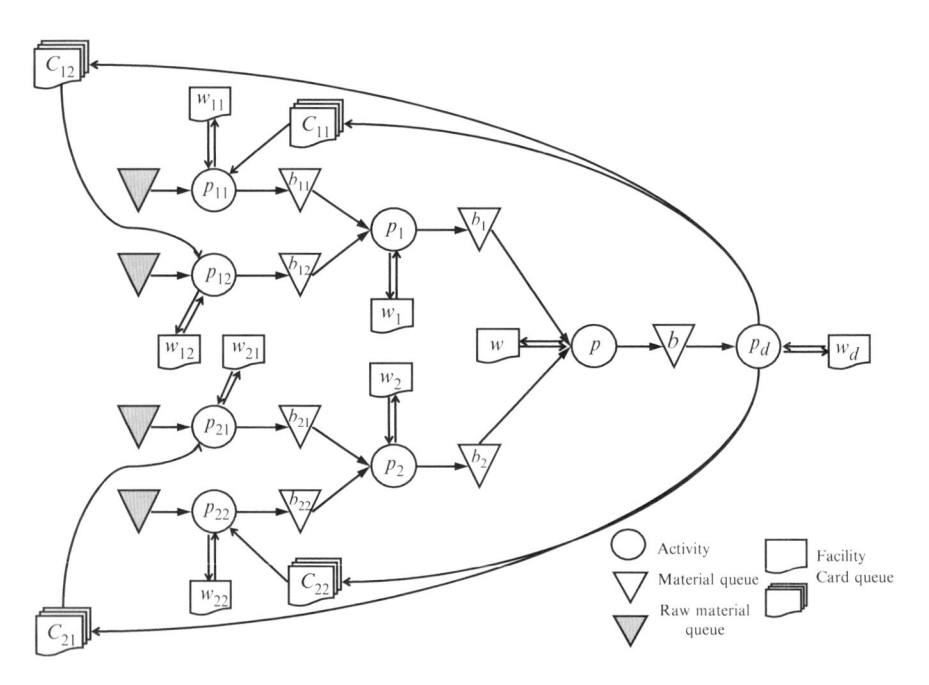

Fig. 6.2 The assembly production process in Fig. 6.1 controlled by CONWIP

6.1 Analysis of Kanban and CONWIP

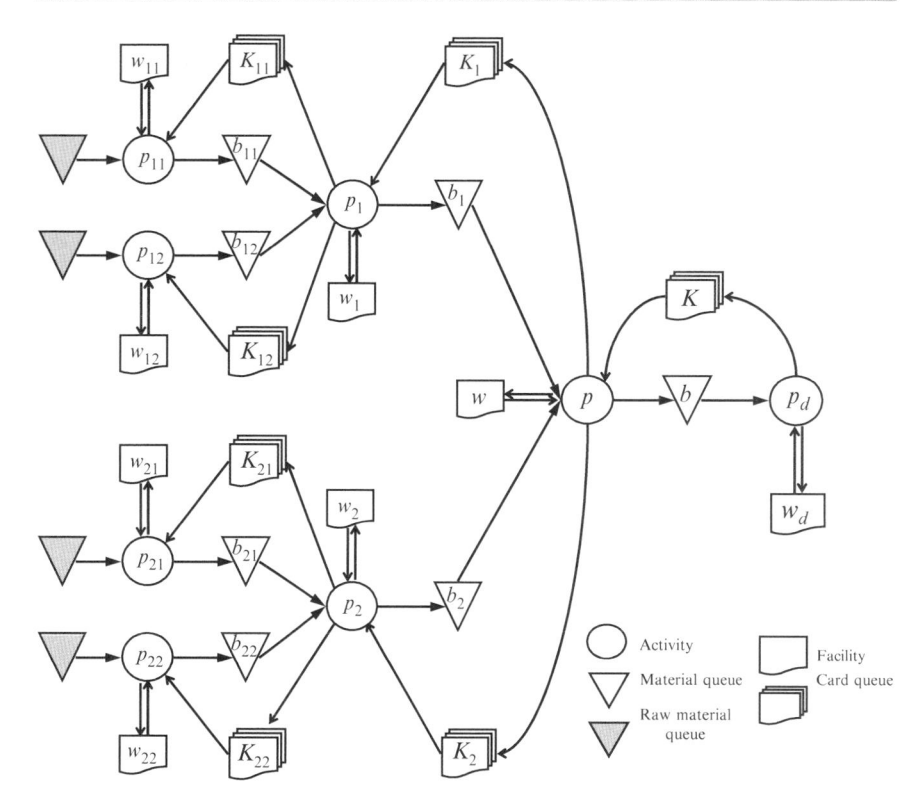

Fig. 6.3 The assembly production process in Fig. 6.1 controlled by Kanban

decide the throughput and optimality of the system WIP. All of the following four cases have minimum WIP with respect to throughputs.

Example 6.1: Case *Assembly-CONWIP-1* Processing times of p_{11}, p_{12}, p_{21}, p_{22}, p_1, p_2 and p are set at 8, 11, 6, 15, 9, 12, and 5 time units, respectively. The process p_{22} has two workers, while each of the others has only one worker. Also, initial inventory for every part is set to zero. We assume that enough raw materials are always available. Initial deployments of cards are as follows.

$$c_{11} = c_{12} = c_{21} = 2, \quad \text{and}$$
$$c_{22} = 3.$$

The whole system shows a periodic behavior every 25 time units as Table 6.1 shows. In the table, worker-queues are omitted, because if an activity p_{11}, for example, is in process, then w_{11} is zero.

Example 6.2: Case *Assembly-CONWIP-2* Now, we increase one card in C_{12}. That is, the initial cards are as follows.

Table 6.1 State transition of the case Assembly-CONWIP-1 for a period

Time	C_{11}	p_{11}	b_{11}	C_{12}	p_{12}	b_{12}	p_1	b_1	C_{21}	p_{21}	b_{21}	C_{22}	p_{22}	b_{22}	p_2	b_2	p	b	p_d
82	0	1(8)	0	0	1(11)	0	1(7)	0	0	1(6)	0	0	1(15), 1(2)	0	1(5)	0	---	0	1(12)
84	0	1(6)	0	0	1(9)	0	1(5)	0	0	1(4)	0	0	1(13), ---	1	1(3)	0	---	0	1(10)
87	0	1(3)	0	0	1(6)	0	1(2)	0	0	1(1)	0	0	1(10), ---	1	---	1	---	0	1(7)
88	0	1(2)	0	0	1(5)	0	1(1)	0	0	---	0	0	1(9), ---	0	1(12)	1	---	0	1(6)
89	0	1(1)	0	0	1(4)	0	---	0	0	---	0	0	1(8), ---	0	1(11)	0	1(5)	0	1(5)
90	0	---	0	0	1(3)	0	---	0	0	---	0	0	1(7), ---	0	1(10)	0	1(4)	0	1(4)
93	0	---	0	0	---	0	1(9)	0	0	---	0	0	1(4), ---	0	1(7)	0	1(1)	0	1(1)
94	0	1(8)	0	0	1(11)	0	1(8)	0	0	1(6)	0	0	1(3), 1(15)	0	1(6)	0	---	0	1(12)
97	0	1(5)	0	0	1(8)	0	1(5)	0	0	1(3)	0	0	---, 1(12)	1	1(3)	0	---	0	1(9)
100	0	1(2)	0	0	1(5)	0	1(2)	0	0	---	0	0	---, 1(9)	0	1(12)	1	---	0	1(6)
102	0	---	0	0	1(3)	0	---	0	0	---	0	0	---, 1(7)	0	1(10)	0	1(5)	0	1(4)
105	0	---	0	0	---	0	1(9)	0	0	---	0	0	---, 1(4)	0	1(7)	0	1(2)	0	1(1)
106	0	---	0	0	---	0	1(8)	0	0	---	0	0	---, 1(3)	0	1(6)	0	1(1)	0	---
107	0	1(8)	0	0	1(11)	0	1(7)	0	0	1(6)	0	0	1(15), 1(2)	0	1(5)	0	---	0	1(12)

6.1 Analysis of Kanban and CONWIP

$$c_{11} = c_{21} = 2, \quad \text{and}$$
$$c_{12} = c_{22} = 3.$$

The whole system shows a periodic behavior every 12 time units which is shown in Table 6.2.

Both cases above show a complicated situation in finding the optimal deployment of cards in CONWIP on the same production process. When we increase WIP, for example, the former critical circuit becomes non-critical and another circuit is now critical with a different throughput, and this WIP is still minimum to attain the throughput.

Example 6.3: Case *Assembly-CONWIP-3* The respective processing times of p_{21} and p_{22} have changed here. They changed from 6 and 15 respectively to 8 and 20, while the other processing times as well as the initial inventories remained the same. Respective number of workers also remains the same. Allocated number of cards are $c_{11} = 2$, $c_{12} = c_{21} = 3$, and $c_{12} = 4$. The whole system shows a periodic behavior every 12 time units as well, which is given in Table 6.3. This case will be used later for comparison between CONWIP and Kanban.

Consider the case Assembly-CONWIP-1, and the circuit $C_{12}p_{12}b_{12}p_1b_1pbC_{12}$ in Fig. 6.2. This circuit is critical. In fact, by observing its state transition table given in Table 6.1, we see that every activity on the circuit starts twice in a period, and there are two tokens on average on the circuit at any given time. Since the sum of the processing times on the circuit is 25 ($p_{12} = 11$, $p_1 = 9$, and $p = 5$), the maximum cycle mean is $\lambda = 25/2 = 12.5$. Given the maximum cycle mean, the system throughput can be calculated.[1] Therefore, the throughput of the circuit and the whole system is $1/12.5 = 0.08$ token per time unit.

In the both cases of Assembly-CONWIP-2 and Assembly-CONWIP-3, the critical circuit is $p_2w_2p_2$. That is, p_2 is a critical activity. The period is 12 time units, and the throughput is 1/12 token per time unit. The respective placements of system WIP are optimum for this throughput. The system WIP of the case Assembly-CONWIP-2 is 10.33, while that of Assembly-CONWIP-3 is 11.75. In the following, for the former case, we show how to calculate the system WIP using its state transition table for a period.

Consider Table 6.2. We can count tokens in the places of activity circuits and those in the rest of the places, separately. The number of tokens on an activity circuit is unchanged from the initial state, which is the number of workers of the activity (Sato and Kawai 2007). On the activity circuit p_{22}, for example, there are two tokens. It means that the WIP on this activity circuit is 2. Let the sum of the WIPs on all of activity circuits be denoted by W_A. Since there are eight activities and p_{22} has two workers, we have $W_A = 9$. Now, let us count the tokens in the rest of the places, which are actually connecting queues. Take b_{12} as such an example. By

---

[1] The maximum cycle mean is the reciprocal of the system throughput; that is, TH $= \lambda^{-1}$ (Sato and Khojasteh-Ghamari 2012).

Table 6.2 State transition of the case Assembly-CONWIP-2 for a period

Time	C_{11}	p_{11}	b_{11}	C_{12}	p_{12}	b_{12}	p_1	b_1	C_{21}	p_{21}	b_{21}	C_{22}	p_{22}	b_{22}	p_2	b_2	p	b	p_d
80	0	1(8)	0	0	1(11)	1	1(5)	0	0	1(6)	0	0	1(15), 1(3)	0	1(7)	0	---	0	1(12)
83	0	1(5)	0	0	1(8)	1	1(2)	0	0	1(3)	0	0	1(12), ---	1	1(4)	0	---	0	1(9)
85	0	1(3)	0	0	1(6)	1	---	1	0	1(1)	0	0	1(10), ---	1	1(2)	0	---	0	1(7)
86	0	1(2)	0	0	1(5)	1	---	1	0	---	1	0	1(9), ---	1	1(1)	0	---	0	1(6)
87	0	1(1)	0	0	1(4)	1	---	0	0	---	0	0	1(8), ---	0	1(12)	0	1(5)	0	1(5)
88	0	---	0	0	1(3)	0	1(9)	0	0	---	0	0	1(7), ---	0	1(11)	0	1(4)	0	1(4)
91	0	---	0	0	---	1	1(6)	0	0	---	0	0	1(4), ---	0	1(8)	0	1(1)	0	1(1)
92	0	1(8)	0	0	1(11)	1	1(5)	0	0	1(6)	0	0	1(3), 1(15)	0	1(7)	0	---	0	1(12)

6.1 Analysis of Kanban and CONWIP

Table 6.3 State transition of the case Assembly-CONWIP-3 for a period

Time	C_{11}	p_{11}	b_{11}	C_{12}	p_{12}	b_{12}	p_1	b_1	C_{21}	p_{21}	b_{21}	C_{22}	p_{22}	b_{22}	p_2	b_2	p	b	p_d
89	0	1(8)	0	0	1(11)	1	1(5)	0	0	1(8)	1	0	1(8), 1(20)	1	1(7)	0	----	0	1(12)
94	0	1(3)	0	0	1(6)	1	----	1	0	1(3)	1	0	1(3), 1(15)	1	1(2)	0	----	0	1(7)
96	0	1(1)	0	0	1(4)	1	----	0	0	1(1)	0	0	1(1), 1(13)	0	1(12)	0	1(5)	0	1(5)
97	0	----	0	0	1(3)	0	1(9)	0	0	----	1	0	----, 1(12)	1	1(11)	0	1(4)	0	1(4)
100	0	----	0	0	----	1	1(6)	0	0	----	1	0	----, 1(9)	1	1(8)	0	1(1)	0	1(1)
101	0	1(8)	0	0	1(11)	1	1(5)	0	0	1(8)	1	0	1(20), 1(8)	1	1(7)	0	----	0	1(12)

observing the state transition table for a period from time 88 to 91, a token remains in b_{12} for 9 time units. Thus, its integration value for a period is $1 \times 9 = 9$ [tokens × time unit]. Denote the average WIP in all of the connecting queues by W_Q. Since the connecting queues are $C_{11}, b_{11}, C_{12}, b_{12}, b_1, C_{21}, b_{21}, C_{22}, b_{22}, b_2, b$, we can calculate respective integration values for a period L from the table, and add them. Thus, we have

$$W_Q \cdot L = (0+0+0+9+2+0+1+0+4+0+0) = 16.$$

Therefore, the system WIP is

$$W_A + W_Q = 9 + (16/12) = 10.33.$$

An example of Kanban for the assembly production process is as follow.

Example 6.4: Case *Assembly-Kanban* Concerning Fig. 6.3, processing times of $p_{11}, p_{12}, p_{21}, p_{22}, p_1, p_2$ and p are set at 8, 11, 8, 20, 9, 12, and 5 time units, respectively. The process p_{22} has two workers, while each of the others has only one worker. Also, initial inventory for every part is set to zero. We again assume that enough raw materials are always available. Initial cards are set as $k_{11} = k_{12} = k_{21} = k_1 = k_2 = k = 1$ and $k_{22} = 2$. The state transition for a period is given in Table 6.4, where the throughput is 1/12.

The connecting queues are $K_{11}, b_{11}, K_{12}, b_{12}, K_1, b_1, K_{21}, b_{21}, K_{22}, b_{22}, K_2, b_2, K$ and b. Thus, by calculating respective WIP for those queues from Table 6.4, we have

$$W_Q \cdot L = (0+4+0+1+0+3+0+4+0+4+0+0+7+0) = 23.$$

Therefore, the system WIP is

$$W_A + W_Q = 9 + (23/12) = 10.92.$$

6.1.1.2 Analytical Comparison

The following proposition partly resolves the dynamics of the assembly production controls.

Proposition 6.1 (Khojasteh-Ghamari and Sato 2011) Consider the assembly production processes shown in Figs. 6.2 and 6.3 with CONWIP and Kanban. Let N and K be the total number of cards in the CONWIP and Kanban, respectively. Then, we have the following.

(i) If $N - K \leq \dfrac{h_1 + h_2 + 3h}{\lambda}$, then $W_C \leq W_K$,

(ii) If $N = K$, then $W_C < W_K$,

Table 6.4 State transition of the case Assembly-Kanban for a period

Time	K_{11}	p_{11}	b_{11}	K_{12}	p_{12}	b_{12}	K_1	p_1	b_1	K_{21}	p_{21}	b_{21}	K_{22}	p_{22}	b_{22}	K_2	p_2	b_2	K	p	b	p_d
85	0	1(3)	0	0	1(6)	0	0	1(4)	0	0	1(3)	0	0	1(3), 1(15)	0	0	1(7)	0	1	----	0	1(12)
88	0	----	1	0	1(3)	0	0	1(1)	0	0	----	1	0	----, 1(12)	1	0	1(4)	0	1	----	0	1(9)
89	0	----	1	0	1(2)	0	0	----	1	0	----	1	0	----, 1(11)	1	0	1(3)	0	1	----	0	1(8)
91	0	----	1	0	----	1	0	----	1	0	----	1	0	----, 1(9)	1	0	1(1)	0	1	----	0	1(6)
92	0	1(8)	0	0	1(11)	0	0	1(9)	0	0	1(8)	0	0	1(20), 1(8)	0	0	1(12)	0	0	1(5)	0	1(5)
97	0	1(3)	0	0	1(6)	0	0	1(4)	0	0	1(3)	0	0	1(15), 1(3)	0	0	1(7)	0	1	----	0	1(12)

where λ is the maximum cycle mean, and W_C and W_K are the average system WIPs of the CONWIP and Kanban, respectively.

Proof A proof is given in Proposition 6.2, which addresses a general assembly production process with three stages.

For the assembly production process in the above proposition, some CONWIP and Kanban cases, which have the same level of throughput, satisfy the if-condition of (i), and then $W_C < W_K$ certainly holds (see Example 6.5 below). However, this if-condition is not satisfied by Assembly-CONWIP-3 and Assembly-Kanban cases, where the system WIP is 11.75 and 10.92, respectively. That is, the if-condition of the Proposition 6.1 is meaningful, and we would say that CONWIP does not necessarily outperform Kanban.

The following example shows that the if-condition of (i) in Proposition 6.1 is satisfied, and $W_C < W_K$.

Example 6.5 Consider an assembly production process with $m = 2$ and $n_1 = n_2 = 2$ controlled by the CONWIP and Kanban as depicted in Figs. 6.2 and 6.3, respectively. Processing times of p_{11}, p_{12}, p_{21}, p_{22}, p_1, p_2 and p are set at 10, 11, 12, 20, 10, 10, and 2 time units, respectively. That is, $h_{11} = 10, h_{12} = 11, h_{21} = 12, h_{22} = 20, h_1 = 10, h_2 = 10$, and $h = 2$. The process p_{22} has two workers, while each of the others has only one worker. Also, initial inventory for every part is set to zero. We assume that enough raw materials are always available. Cases 6.5_KAN and 6.5_CON below show the periodic behavior of the Kanban and CONWIP, respectively.

Case **6.5_KAN:** Table 6.5 shows the state transition table for a period of the production process with the Kanban. The number of cards are set as $k_{11} = k_{12} = k_{21} = k_1 = k_2 = k = 1$ and $k_{22} = 2$, that is $K = 8$. The system shows a periodic behavior every 12 time units. Circuit $p_{21}w_{21}p_{21}$ is critical with maximum cycle mean $\lambda = 12$. Each activity starts once in a period. The throughput is 1/12, and the system WIP is equal to 10.75. That is, $W_K = 10.75$. It can be verified that the amount of system WIP is minimum to attain the throughput 1/12.

Case **6.5_CON:** The state transition table for a period of the same production process with the CONWIP is given in Table 6.6. The number of cards are set as $c_{11} = c_{12} = c_{21} = 2$ and $c_{22} = 3$, which are the minimum number of cards to attain the maximum possible throughput. The system shows a periodic behavior every 12 time units. The activity circuit $p_{21}w_{21}p_{21}$ is critical with $\lambda = 12$. Each activity starts once in a period. The throughput is 1/12, and the system WIP is equal to 9.50 ($W_C = 9.50$), which is the minimum value to attain the throughput.

Case 6.5_KAN and 6.5_CON show that the if-condition of (i) in Proposition 6.1 is satisfied ($N - K = 9 - 8 < \frac{h_1+h_2+3h}{\lambda} = \frac{10+10+3(2)}{12}$), and we have $W_C < W_K$, in the same notation of Proposition 6.1.

Table 6.5 State transition of 6.5_KAN for a period

Time	K_{11}	b_{11}	p_{11}	b_{11}	K_{12}	p_{12}	b_{12}	K_1	p_1	b_1	K_{21}	p_{21}	b_{21}	K_{22}	p_{22}	b_{22}	K_2	p_2	b_2	K	p	b	p_d
877	0	1	----	1	0	----	1	0	----	1	0	1(3)	0	0	----, 1(11)	1	0	1(1)	0	1	----	0	1(3)
878	0	0	1(10)	0	0	1(11)	0	0	1(10)	0	0	1(2)	0	0	----, 1(10)	1	1	----	0	0	1(2)	0	1(2)
880	0	0	1(8)	0	0	1(9)	0	0	1(8)	0	0	1(12)	0	0	1(20), 1(8)	0	0	1(10)	0	1	----	0	1(12)
888	0	1	----	1	0	1(1)	0	0	----	1	0	1(4)	0	0	1(12), ----	1	0	1(2)	0	1	----	0	1(4)
889	0	1	----	1	0	----	1	0	----	1	0	1(3)	0	0	1(11), ----	1	0	1(1)	0	1	----	0	1(3)

Table 6.6 State transition of the 6.5_CON for a period

Time	C_{11}	p_{11}	b_{11}	C_{12}	p_{12}	b_{12}	p_1	b_1	C_{21}	p_{21}	b_{21}	C_{22}	p_{22}	b_{22}	p_2	b_2	p	b	p_d
880	0	1(10)	0	0	1(11)	0	1(9)	0	0	1(12)	0	0	1(20), 1(8)	0	1(10)	0	---	0	1(12)
888	0	1(2)	0	0	1(3)	0	1(1)	0	0	1(4)	0	0	1(12), ---	1	1(2)	0	---	0	1(4)
889	0	1(1)	0	0	1(2)	0	---	1	0	1(3)	0	0	1(11), ---	1	1(1)	0	---	0	1(3)
890	0	---	1	0	1(1)	0	---	0	0	1(2)	0	0	1(10), ---	1	---	0	1(2)	0	1(2)
891	0	---	0	0	---	0	1(10)	0	0	1(1)	0	0	1(9), ---	1	---	0	1(1)	0	1(1)
892	0	1(10)	0	0	1(11)	0	1(9)	0	0	1(12)	0	0	1(8), 1(20)	0	1(10)	0	---	0	1(12)

6.1.2 Generalized Assembly Production Processes

We generalize the model considered in Proposition 6.1 for a complex production process as depicted in Fig. 6.4. In this figure, we consider a three-stage production process with $m \geq 1$ workstations in stage 2, each of which with n_i ($i = 1, 2, \ldots, m$) workstations in stage 1. Parts are fabricated in the first stage, subassemblies are made in the second, and products are assembled in the third. Production processes were created for fabricating each of the n_i parts for subassembly i in the first stage

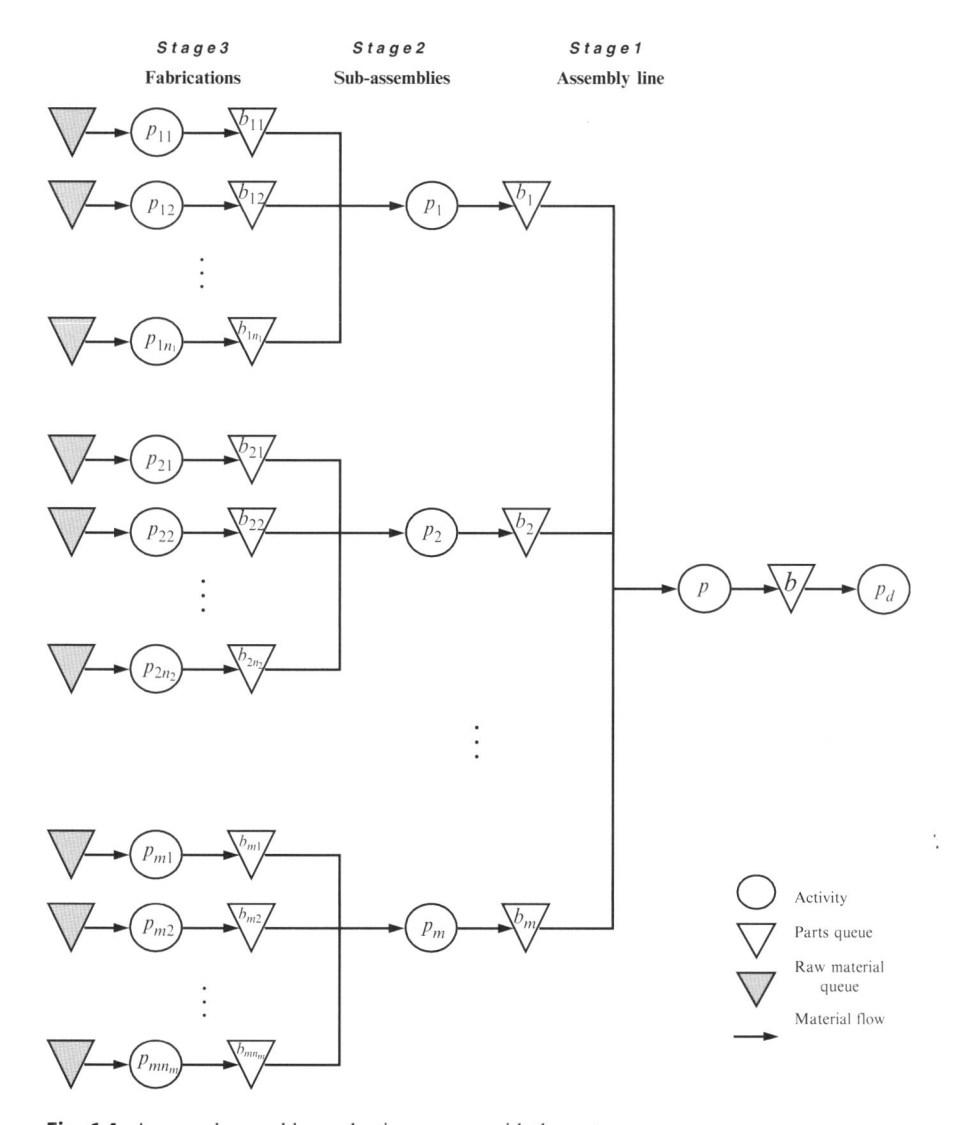

Fig. 6.4 A general assembly production process with three stages

and for each of the m subassemblies in the second stage. In the third stage, a production process was created for assembling the product. Therefore, as we go upstream, the single process for assembling the product branches into the m processes for fabricating each subassembly, and the ith process branches into the n_i processes for fabricating each part.

6.1.2.1 Analytical Comparisons

Proposition 6.2 Consider an assembly production process with $m \geq 1$ workstations in stage 2, each of which with n_i ($i = 1, 2, \ldots, m$) workstations in stage 1 as shown in Fig. 6.4 with the CONWIP and Kanban. Assume that both the systems have the same number of workers for respective processes and the same throughput. Let N and K be the total number of cards in the CONWIP and Kanban, respectively. Then, we have the followings.

(i) If $N - K \leq \dfrac{\sum_{i=1}^{m}(n_i - 1)h_i + h\left(\sum_{i=1}^{m} n_i - 1\right)}{\lambda}$, then $W_C \leq W_K$,

(ii) If $N = K$, then $W_C < W_K$,

where, λ is the maximum cycle mean, h_i the processing time of the process p_i, and W_C and W_K are the average system WIP of the CONWIP and Kanban, respectively.

Proof Consider the assembly production process shown in Fig. 6.4 with $m \geq 1$ and $n_i \geq 1$, $i = 1, 2, \ldots, m$. Let the processing time of p, p_i and p_{ij} ($i = 1, 2, \ldots, m$ and $j = 1, 2, \ldots, n_i$) be h, h_i and h_{ij}, respectively.

(1) Let the throughput be TH, the activation frequency ρ, and the period L. Then, we have $TH = \rho/L$, since every activity starts and ends ρ times in the period, and one token moves at every commencement (or, completion). Thus, both systems have the same period L, and the same maximum cycle mean λ.

(2) Let $\overline{C}$ be a circuit. Tokens are held in activities or connecting queues. We denote $a \in A(\overline{C})$ to show that an activity a is on $\overline{C}$, and $q \in Q(\overline{C})$ if a connecting queue q is on $\overline{C}$. The processing time of a is denoted by h_a. For a connecting queue q, denote the integration value of token in the queue for a period as h_q. Thus, the average WIP in q is h_q/L. The sum of integration value of connecting queues on $\overline{C}$ is $\sum_{q \in Q(\overline{C})} h_q$. As we showed in the proof of Proposition 5.1,

$$n_C \cdot L = \rho \left(\sum_{a \in A(\overline{C})} h_a \right) + \sum_{q \in Q(\overline{C})} h_q$$

holds for an arbitrary circuit $\overline{C}$, where n_C is the number of tokens on the circuit.

6.1 Analysis of Kanban and CONWIP

(3) The sum of integration values of connecting queues on all *activity circuits* in both CONWIP and Kanban for a period is the same. In the CONWIP, let the integration value of a token in the worker for p_{ij} ($i = 1, 2, \ldots, m$ and $j = 1, 2, \ldots, n_i$) be $h_{q_{ij}}^C$. Then, we have $h_{q_{ij}}^C = w_{ij} \cdot L - \rho \cdot h_{ij}$, where w_{ij} is the number of workers for p_{ij}. Since the right-hand side is identical for the Kanban, we have $h_{q_{ij}}^C = h_{q_{ij}}^K$, where $h_{q_{ij}}^K$ is the integration value of the process p_{ij} in the Kanban. Similarly, the integration values of the process p_i in both Kanban and CONWIP are the same (i.e., $h_{q_i}^C = h_{q_i}^K$). Similarly, we have $h_q^C = h_q^K$, where h_q^C and h_q^K are the integration values of the process p in the CONWIP and Kanban, respectively. In the following, the sum of integration values of all activity circuits for a period is denoted by w. That is,

$$w = \sum_{i=1}^{m} \sum_{j=1}^{n_i} h_{q_{ij}}^C + \sum_{i=1}^{m} h_{q_i}^C + h_q^C = \sum_{i=1}^{m} \sum_{j=1}^{n_i} h_{q_{ij}}^K + \sum_{i=1}^{m} h_{q_i}^K + h_q^K. \quad (6.1)$$

(4) The CONWIP and Kanban have respectively $\sum_{i=1}^{m} n_i$ and $\sum_{i=1}^{m} n_i + m + 1$ elementary circuits[2] other than their activity circuits for the same process structure. In the CONWIP, let $\overline{C}_{ij}$ ($i = 1, 2, \ldots, m$ and $j = 1, 2, \ldots, n_i$) be the circuit $C_{ij} p_{ij} b_{ij} p_i b_i p b C_{ij}$ with c_{ij} tokens. In the Kanban, let D_{ij} ($i = 1, 2, \ldots, m$ and $j = 1, 2, \ldots, n_i$) be the circuit $K_{ij} p_{ij} b_{ij} K_{ij}$ with k_{ij} tokens. Also, let D_i ($i = 1, 2, \ldots, m$) and D be the circuit $K_i p_i b_i K_i$ with k_i tokens, and the circuit $KpbK$ with k tokens, respectively.

(5) In the CONWIP, the sum of integration values of tokens in circuit $\overline{C}_{ij}$ for a period is given by $\sum_{q \in Q(\overline{C}_{ij})} h_q = c_{ij} \cdot L - \rho \left(\sum_{a \in A(\overline{C}_{ij})} h_a \right)$. In the Kanban, however, the integration value of tokens in circuits D_{ij}, D_i and D is given by $h_{q_{ij}} = k_{ij} \cdot L - \rho \cdot h_{ij}$, $h_{q_i} = k_i \cdot L - \rho \cdot h_i$. and $h_q = k \cdot L - \rho \cdot h$, respectively. Let the sum of the integration values of all connecting queues in CONWIP and Kanban for a period be W_q^C and W_q^K, respectively. Then,

$$W_q^C \leq \sum_{q \in Q(\overline{C}_{11})} h_q + \sum_{q \in Q(\overline{C}_{12})} h_q + \ldots + \sum_{q \in Q(\overline{C}_{mn_m})} h_q + w \quad (6.2)$$

$$= [c_{11} \cdot L - \rho(h_{11} + h_1 + h)] + [c_{12} \cdot L - \rho(h_{12} + h_1 + h)] + \ldots + [c_{mn_m} \cdot L - \rho(h_{mn_m} + h_m + h)] + w$$

---

[2] An elementary circuit is a circuit that contains different activities and queues (except the start and end one).

$$= (c_{11} + c_{12} + \ldots + c_{mn_m})L - \rho(h_{11} + h_{12} + \ldots + h_{1n_1} + h_{21} + h_{22} + \ldots$$
$$+ h_{2n_2} + \ldots + h_{m1} + h_{m2} + \ldots + h_{mn_m} n_1 h_1 + n_2 h_2 + \ldots + n_m h_m + h \sum_{i=1}^{m} n_i) + w$$

$$= \left(\sum_{i=1}^{m}\sum_{j=1}^{n_i} c_{ij}\right)L - \rho\left(\sum_{i=1}^{m}\sum_{j=1}^{n_i} h_{ij} + \sum_{i=1}^{m} n_i h_i + \sum_{i=1}^{m} n_i h\right) + w. \tag{6.3}$$

And,

$$W_q^K = \sum_{q \in Q(D_{11})} h_q + \sum_{q \in Q(D_{12})} h_q + \ldots + \sum_{q \in Q(D_{1n_1})} h_q + \sum_{q \in Q(D_{21})} h_q + \sum_{q \in Q(D_{22})} h_q$$
$$+ \ldots + \sum_{q \in Q(D_{2n_2})} h_q + \sum_{q \in Q(D_{m1})} h_q + \sum_{q \in Q(D_{m2})} h_q + \ldots$$
$$+ \sum_{q \in Q(D_{mn_m})} h_q + \sum_{q \in Q(D_1)} h_q + \sum_{q \in Q(D_2)} h_q + \ldots$$
$$+ \sum_{q \in Q(D_m)} h_q + \sum_{q \in Q(D)} h_q + w$$
$$\tag{6.4}$$

$$= [k_{11}L - \rho h_{11}] + [k_{12}L - \rho h_{12}] + \ldots + [k_{1n_1}L - \rho h_{1n_1}] +$$
$$[k_{21}L - \rho h_{21}] + [k_{22}L - \rho h_{22}] + \ldots + [k_{2n_2}L - \rho h_{2n_2}] + \ldots +$$
$$[k_{m1}L - \rho h_{m1}] + [k_{m2}L - \rho h_{m2}] + \ldots + [k_{mn_m}L - \rho h_{mn_m}] +$$
$$[k_1 L - \rho h_1] + [k_2 L - \rho h_2] + \ldots + [k_m L - \rho h_m] + [kL - \rho h] + w$$

$$= \left(\sum_{i=1}^{m}\sum_{j=1}^{n_i} k_{ij} + \sum_{i=1}^{m} k_i + k\right)L - \rho\left(\sum_{i=1}^{m}\sum_{j=1}^{n_i} h_{ij} + \sum_{i=1}^{m} h_i + h\right) + w. \tag{6.5}$$

Note that inequality used in (6.2) is because of the existence of some common activities and connecting queues among the elementary circuits in the CONWIP. N and K are represented as follows.

$$N = \sum_{i=1}^{m}\sum_{j=1}^{n_i} c_{ij}, \quad \text{and} \quad K = \sum_{i=1}^{m}\sum_{j=1}^{n_i} k_{ij} + \sum_{i=1}^{m} k_i + k. \tag{6.6}$$

Therefore, (6.3) and (6.5) can be respectively written as

$$W_q^C \leq N \cdot L - \rho\left(\sum_{i=1}^{m}\sum_{j=1}^{n_i} h_{ij} + \sum_{i=1}^{m} n_i h_i + \sum_{i=1}^{m} n_i h\right) + w, \quad \text{and} \tag{6.7}$$

6.1 Analysis of Kanban and CONWIP

$$W_q^K = K \cdot L - \rho \left(\sum_{i=1}^{m} \sum_{j=1}^{n_i} h_{ij} + \sum_{i=1}^{m} h_i + h \right) + w. \tag{6.8}$$

Now, subtracting W_q^K in (6.8) from the both sides of (6.7), yields

$$W_q^C - W_q^K \leq (N - K)L - \rho \left(\sum_{i=1}^{m} (n_i - 1)h_i + h \left(\sum_{i=1}^{m} n_i - 1 \right) \right). \tag{6.9}$$

If $N - K \leq \dfrac{\sum_{i=1}^{m}(n_i - 1)h_i + h\left(\sum_{i=1}^{m} n_i - 1\right)}{\lambda}$, then

$(N - K)L - \rho \left(\sum_{i=1}^{m}(n_i - 1)h_i + h \left(\sum_{i=1}^{m} n_i - 1 \right) \right) \leq 0$. By (6.9),

$$W_q^C - W_q^K \leq (N - K)L - \rho \left(\sum_{i=1}^{m}(n_i - 1)h_i + h \left(\sum_{i=1}^{m} n_i - 1 \right) \right) \leq 0, \text{ or } W_q^C \leq W_q^K.$$

Therefore,

$$W_C = \frac{\rho}{L} \left(\sum_{a \in A} h_a \right) + \frac{1}{L} W_q^C \leq \frac{\rho}{L} \left(\sum_{a \in A} h_a \right) + \frac{1}{L} W_q^K = W_K.$$

Thus, $W_C \leq W_K$. This concludes the proof of part (i).

(6) Now we prove part (ii). If $K = N$, i.e., the total number of cards assigned to the Kanban be the same as that assigned to the CONWIP, then in (6.9) by assuming that there exist an $i \in \{1, \ldots, m\}$ such that $n_i > 1$, we have

$$W_q^K - W_q^C \geq \rho \left(\sum_{i=1}^{m}(n_i - 1)h_i + h \left(\sum_{i=1}^{m} n_i - 1 \right) \right) > 0, \text{ or } W_q^C < W_q^K.$$

Thus, $W_C < W_K$. (Q.E.D.)

In order for the above proof to be followed more simply, in the following, we rewrite some of the equalities and inequalities given in the proof, but for a more simple assembly production process, where $m = 2$ and $n_1 = n_2 = 2$ (this production process is depicted in Figs. 6.2 and 6.3 with CONWIP and Kanban, respectively). Equation (6. *)′ is the simplified form of Equation (6.*).

$$w = h^C_{q_{11}} + h^C_{q_{12}} + h^C_{q_{21}} + h^C_{q_{22}} + h^C_{q_1} + h^C_{q_2} + h^C_q$$
$$= h^K_{q_{11}} + h^K_{q_{12}} + h^K_{q_{21}} + h^K_{q_{22}} + h^K_{q_1} + h^K_{q_2} + h^K_q. \quad (6.1')$$

$$W^C_q \leq \sum_{q \in Q(\bar{C}_{11})} h_q + \sum_{q \in Q(\bar{C}_{12})} h_q + \sum_{q \in Q(\bar{C}_{21})} h_q + \sum_{q \in Q(\bar{C}_{22})} h_q + w. \quad (6.2')$$

$$= [c_{11} \cdot L - \rho(h_{11} + h_1 + h)] + [c_{12} \cdot L - \rho(h_{12} + h_1 + h)] +$$
$$[c_{21} \cdot L - \rho(h_{21} + h_2 + h)] + [c_{22} \cdot L - \rho(h_{22} + h_2 + h)] + w.$$

$$= (c_{11} + c_{12} + c_{21} + c_{22})L - \rho(h_{11} + h_{12} + h_{21} + h_{22} + 2h_1 + 2h_2 + 4h) + w. \quad (6.3')$$

$$W^K_q = \sum_{q \in Q(D_{11})} h_q + \sum_{q \in Q(D_{12})} h_q + \sum_{q \in Q(D_{21})} h_q + \sum_{q \in Q(D_{22})} h_q + \sum_{q \in Q(D_1)} h_q$$
$$+ \sum_{q \in Q(D_2)} h_q + \sum_{q \in Q(D)} h_q + w. \quad (6.4')$$

$$= [k_{11}L - \rho h_{11}] + [k_{12}L - \rho h_{12}] + [k_{21}L - \rho h_{21}] + [k_{22}L - \rho h_{22}] +$$
$$[k_1 L - \rho h_1] + [k_2 L - \rho h_2] + [kL - \rho h] + w$$

$$= (k_{11} + k_{12} + k_{21} + k_{22} + k_1 + k_2 + k)L$$
$$- \rho(h_{11} + h_{12} + h_{21} + h_{22} + h_1 + h_2 + h) + w \quad (6.5')$$

$$N = c_{11} + c_{12} + c_{21} + c_{22}, \text{ and}$$
$$K = k_{11} + k_{12} + k_{21} + k_{22} + k_1 + k_2 + k \quad (6.6')$$

$$W^C_q \leq N \cdot L - \rho(h_{11} + h_{12} + h_{21} + h_{22} + 2h_1 + 2h_2 + 4h) + w \quad (6.7')$$

$$W^K_q = K \cdot L - \rho(h_{11} + h_{12} + h_{21} + h_{22} + h_1 + h_2 + h) + w \quad (6.8')$$

$$W^C_q - W^K_q \leq (N - K)L - \rho(h_1 + h_2 + 3h) \quad (6.9')$$

6.1.2.2 Discussions

The statement (i) in Proposition 6.2 implies that if the optimum number of cards[3] in both the control systems satisfies the condition, which does not depend on the processing times in stage 1 (h_{ij}), then $W_C \leq W_K$. In fact, the right hand side is decided by the structure of the process. Once it is given, the whole performance is decided only by the number of cards, N and K. Also, this proposition is one of the best possible forms in the sense that the respective converses do not hold true. It suffices to show that there exists at least an example for the converse. The following example shows that each converse implications of (i) and (ii) in Proposition 6.2

---

[3] The optimal number of cards in a control system is the least total number of cards employed in the system to attain the maximum possible throughput.

6.1 Analysis of Kanban and CONWIP

does not hold. (Assumptions and parameters considered in Examples 6.6, 6.7, and 6.8 are given in Table 6.16.)

Example 6.6 Consider an assembly production process with $m = 2$ and $n_1 = n_2 = 2$ controlled by the CONWIP and Kanban as depicted in Figs. 6.2 and 6.3, respectively. Processing times of p_{11}, p_{12}, p_{21}, p_{22}, p_1, p_2 and p are set at 10, 11, 12, 20, 4, 4 and 1 time units, respectively. That is, $h_{11} = 10$, $h_{12} = 11$, $h_{21} = 12$, $h_{22} = 20$, $h_1 = 4$, $h_2 = 4$, and $h = 1$. The process p_{22} has two workers, while each of the others has only one worker. Also, initial inventory for every part is set to zero. We assume that enough raw materials are always available. Cases 6.6_KAN and 6.6_CON below show the periodic behavior of the Kanban and CONWIP, respectively.

Case **6.6_KAN:** Table 6.7 shows the state transition table for a period of the production process with the Kanban. Initial cards are set as $k_{11} = k_{12} = k_{21} = k_1 = k_2 = k = 1$ and $k_{22} = 2$, that is $K = 8$. The system shows a periodic behavior every 12 time units. Activity circuit $p_{21}w_{21}p_{21}$ is critical with maximum cycle mean $\lambda = 12$. Each activity starts once in a period. The throughput is 1/12, and the system WIP is equal to 11.83. That is, $W_K = 11.83$. It can be verified that the amount of system WIP is minimum to attain the throughput 1/12.[4]

Case **6.6_CON:** The state transition table for a period of the same production process with the CONWIP is given in Table 6.8. Initial cards are set as $c_{11} = c_{12} = c_{21} = 2$ and $c_{22} = 3$, which are the minimum number of cards to attain the maximum possible throughput. The system shows a periodic behavior every 12 time units. Circuit $p_{21}w_{21}p_{21}$ is critical with $\lambda = 12$. Each activity starts once in a period. The throughput is 1/12, and the system WIP is equal to 11.25 ($W_C = 11.25$), which is the minimum value to attain the throughput.

The system WIPs of the CONWIP and Kanban in Example 6.6 are calculated as follows. Consider Table 6.8. We can count tokens in the places of activity circuits and those in the rest of the places, separately. The number of tokens on an activity circuit is unchanged from the initial state, which is the number of workers for the activity. On the activity circuit p_{22}, for example, there are two tokens. It means that the WIP on this activity circuit is 2. Here, let us denote the sum of WIP on all of the activity circuits by W_A. Since there are eight activities, and p_{22} has two workers, we have $W_A = 9$. Now, let us count tokens in the rest of the places, which are actually connecting queues. Take b_1 as an example. By observing the state transition table for a period from time 760 to 772, one token remains in b_1 for 8 time units (771–763 = 8). Thus, its integration value for a period is $1 \times 8 = 8$ [tokens × time unit]. Denote the average WIP in all of the connecting queues by W_Q. Since the

---
[4]The calculation method of the system WIP and maximum cycle mean of this example is presented later in this section.

Table 6.7 State transition of 6.6_KAN for a period

Time	K_{11}	p_{11}	b_{11}	K_{12}	p_{12}	b_{12}	K_1	p_1	b_1	K_{21}	p_{21}	b_{21}	K_{22}	p_{22}	b_{22}	K_2	p_2	b_2	K	p	b	p_d
763	0	1(10)	0	0	1(11)	0	0	1(4)	0	0	1(8)	0	0	1(16), 1(4)	0	1	----	0	0	1(1)	0	1(1)
764	0	1(9)	0	0	1(10)	0	0	1(3)	0	0	1(7)	0	0	1(15), 1(3)	0	1	----	0	1	----	0	1(12)
767	0	1(6)	0	0	1(7)	0	0	----	1	0	1(4)	0	0	1(12), ----	1	1	----	0	1	----	0	1(9)
771	0	1(2)	0	0	1(3)	0	0	----	1	0	1(12)	0	0	1(8), 1(20)	0	0	1(4)	0	1	----	0	1(5)
773	0	----	1	0	1(1)	0	0	----	1	0	1(10)	0	0	1(6), 1(18)	0	0	1(2)	0	1	----	0	1(3)
774	0	----	1	0	----	1	0	----	1	0	1(9)	0	0	1(5), 1(17)	0	0	1(1)	0	1	----	0	1(2)
775	0	1(10)	0	0	1(11)	0	0	1(4)	0	0	1(8)	0	0	1(4), 1(16)	0	1	----	0	0	1(1)	0	1(1)

6.1 Analysis of Kanban and CONWIP

Table 6.8 State transition of the 6.6_CON for a period

Time	C_{11}	p_{11}	b_{11}	C_{12}	p_{12}	b_{12}	p_1	b_1	C_{21}	p_{21}	b_{21}	C_{22}	p_{22}	b_{22}	p_2	b_2	p	b	p_d
760	0	1(10)	0	0	1(11)	0	1(3)	0	1	1(7)	0	0	1(8), 1(20)	1	----	0	----	0	1(12)
763	0	1(7)	0	0	1(8)	0	----	1	1	1(4)	0	0	1(5), 1(17)	1	----	0	----	0	1(9)
767	0	1(3)	0	0	1(4)	0	----	1	0	1(12)	0	0	1(1), 1(13)	0	1(4)	0	----	0	1(5)
768	0	1(2)	0	0	1(3)	0	----	1	0	1(11)	0	0	----, 1(12)	1	1(3)	0	----	0	1(4)
770	0	----	1	0	1(1)	0	----	1	0	1(9)	0	0	----, 1(10)	1	1(1)	0	----	0	1(2)
771	0	----	0	0	----	0	1(4)	0	0	1(8)	0	0	----, 1(9)	1	----	0	1(1)	0	1(1)
772	0	1(10)	0	0	1(11)	0	1(3)	0	1	1(7)	0	0	1(20), 1(8)	1	----	0	----	0	1(12)

Table 6.9 Cycle means in the CONWIP

Circuit no.	Circuit in CONWIP	Sum of processing times	Number of tokens in the circuit	Cycle mean
1	$C_{11}p_{11}b_{11}p_1b_1pbC_{11}$	$10+4+1=15$	2	$15/2 = 7.5$
2	$C_{12}p_{12}b_{12}p_1b_1pbC_{12}$	$11+4+1=16$	2	$16/2 = 8$
3	$C_{21}p_{21}b_{21}p_2b_2pbC_{21}$	$12+4+1=17$	2	$17/2 = 8.5$
4	$C_{22}p_{22}b_{22}p_2b_2pbC_{22}$	$20+4+1=25$	3	$25/3 = 8.33$
5	$p_{11}w_{11}p_{11}$	10	1	10
6	$p_{12}w_{12}p_{12}$	11	1	11
7	$p_1w_1p_1$	4	1	4
8	$p_{21}w_{21}p_{21}$	12	1	12
9	$p_{22}w_{22}p_{22}$	20	2	$20/2 = 10$
10	$p_2w_2p_2$	4	1	4
11	pwp	1	1	1

connecting queues are $C_{11}, b_{11}, C_{12}, b_{12}, b_1, C_{21}, b_{21}, C_{22}, b_{22}, b_2$ and b, we can calculate respective integration values for a period L from the table, and add them. Thus, we have

$$W_Q \cdot L = (0+1+0+0+8+7+0+0+11+0+0) = 27.$$

Therefore, the system WIP is $W_A + W_Q = 9 + (27/12) = 11.25$. That is, $W_C = 11.25$.

In the Kanban, the connecting queues are $K_{11}, b_{11}, K_{12}, b_{12}, K_1, b_1, K_{21}, b_{21}, K_{22}, b_{22}, K_2, b_2, K$ and b. Thus, by calculating the respective value of WIP for those queues from Table 6.7, we have

$$W_Q \cdot L = (0+2+0+1+0+8+0+0+0+4+8+0+11+0) = 34.$$

Therefore, the system WIP is $W_K = W_A + W_Q = 9 + (34/12) = 11.83$.

Now we show how to calculate the maximum cycle means in Example 6.6. There are 11 and 14 circuits in the CONWIP and Kanban, respectively (see Figs. 6.2 and 6.3). The cycle means of all circuits in the CONWIP are calculated as shown in Table 6.9. The maximum cycle mean is 12, which is for the critical circuit $p_{21}w_{21}p_{21}$ (circuit number 8).

The cycle means of all circuits in the Kanban can be calculated in the same way as shown in Table 6.10. The maximum cycle mean of the Kanban is 12, which is for the critical circuits $K_{21}p_{21}b_{21}K_{21}$ and $p_{21}w_{21}p_{21}$ with circuit numbers 4 and 11, respectively.

Notice that all the activity circuits in the CONWIP and Kanban are identical having the same cycle mean (the last seven circuits in Tables 6.9 and 6.10).

Case 6.6_KAN and 6.6_CON show that each converse implications of (i) and (ii) in Proposition 6.2 does not hold. Because it can be simply verified that $W_C < W_K$, however, $N \neq K$, and also $N - K = 9 - 8 > \frac{h_1 + h_2 + 3h}{\lambda} = \frac{4+4+3(1)}{12}$.

Table 6.10 Cycle means in the Kanban

Circuit no.	Circuit in Kanban	Sum of processing times	Number of tokens in the circuit	Cycle mean
1	$K_{11}p_{11}b_{11}K_{11}$	10	1	10
2	$K_{12}p_{12}b_{12}K_{12}$	11	1	11
3	$K_1 p_1 b_1 K_1$	4	1	4
4	$K_{21}p_{21}b_{21}K_{21}$	12	1	12
5	$K_{22}p_{22}b_{22}K_{22}$	20	2	$20/2 = 10$
6	$K_2 p_2 b_2 K_2$	4	1	4
7	$KpbK$	1	1	1
8	$p_{11}w_{11}p_{11}$	10	1	10
9	$p_{12}w_{12}p_{12}$	11	1	11
10	$p_1 w_1 p_1$	4	1	4
11	$p_{21}w_{21}p_{21}$	12	1	12
12	$p_{22}w_{22}p_{22}$	20	2	$20/2 = 10$
13	$p_2 w_2 p_2$	4	1	4
14	pwp	1	1	1

6.2 Comparison of Kanban and Base-stock

Figure 6.5 shows the assembly production process (depicted in Fig. 6.1) controlled by the Base-stock. This control system is specified as follows. Let p_{ij} be any one of p_{11}, p_{12}, p_{21} and p_{22}. In order to start processing for p_{ij}, more than one token should exist in each of w_{ij} and B_{ij}. When it starts, one token is decreased from each of them, and one token is being processed in p_{ij}. We assume enough raw materials as well. After its holding time elapsed and it finishes the processing, the token in p_{ij} is removed, and one token is added to each of b_{ij} and w_{ij}. The process p_1 starts when more than one token exist in each of the input b_{11}, b_{12}, w_1 and B_1. When p_1 starts, those tokens are respectively removed, and one token is being processed in p_1. When p_1 finishes, one token is added into each of b_1 and w_1. The activities p_2 and p work similarly. The delivery process, p_d, starts when more than one token exist in each of b and w_d. It outputs one token into each of B, B_i and B_{ij} at the commencement, and one token in w_d at the end of its process.

In the following section, we present an analytical comparison between Kanban and Base-stock in the assembly production process depicted in Fig. 6.4.

6.2.1 Analytical Comparison

Proposition 6.3 Consider an assembly production process with $m \geq 1$ workstations in stage 2, each of which with n_i ($i = 1, 2, \ldots, m$) workstations in stage 1 as shown in Fig. 6.4 with Kanban and Base-stock. Let K and B be the total number of cards in the Kanban and Base-stock, respectively. Then, we have the followings.

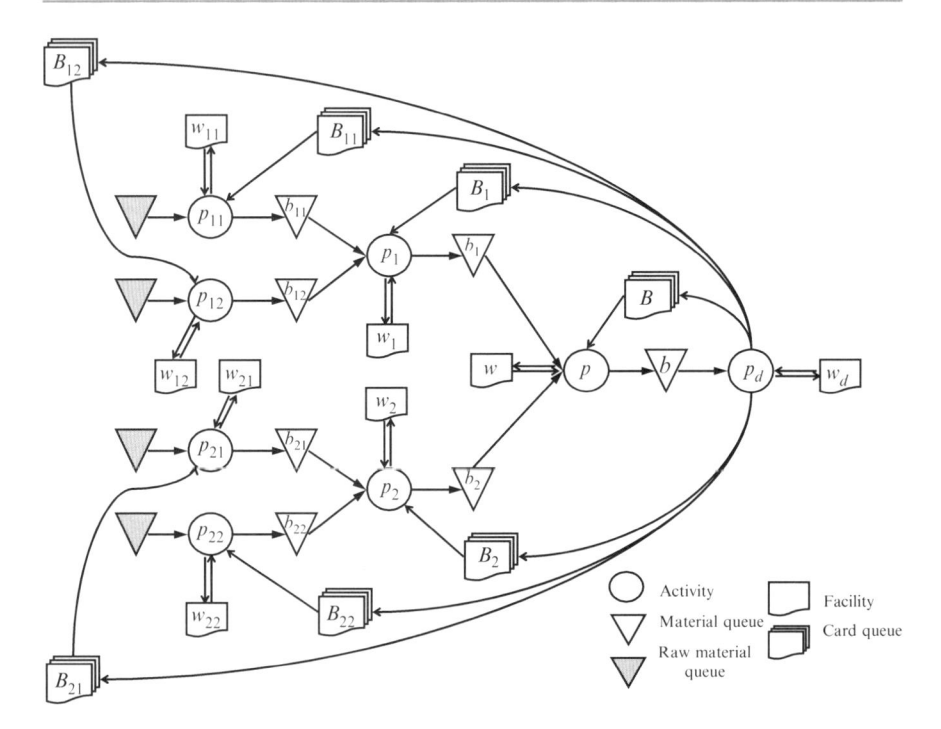

Fig. 6.5 The assembly production process in Fig. 6.1 controlled by Base-stock

(i) If $B - K \leq \dfrac{\sum_{i=1}^{m} n_i h_i + h\left(\sum_{i=1}^{m} n_i + m\right)}{\lambda}$, then $W_B \leq W_K$,

(ii) If $B = K$, then $W_B < W_K$,

where, λ is the maximum cycle mean, h_i the processing time of the process p_i, and W_K and W_B are the average system WIP of the Kanban and Base-stock, respectively.

Proof Consider the assembly production process shown in Fig. 6.4 with $m \geq 1$ and $n_i \geq 1$, $i = 1, 2, \ldots, m$. Let the processing time of p, p_i and p_{ij} ($i = 1, 2, \ldots, m$ and $j = 1, 2, \ldots, n_i$) be h, h_i and h_{ij}, respectively.

(1) Let the throughput be *TH*, the activation frequency ρ, and the period L. As shown in the proof of Proposition 6.2, both systems have the same period, and hence the same maximum cycle mean λ. Also, for an arbitrary circuit $\overline{C}$, we have $n_{\overline{C}} \cdot L = \rho\left(\sum_{a \in A(\overline{C})} h_a\right) + \sum_{q \in Q(\overline{C})} h_q$, where $n_{\overline{C}}$ is the number of tokens on $\overline{C}$, and h_a and h_q are the processing time of activity a, and the integration value of token in the connecting queue q for a period, respectively.

6.2 Comparison of Kanban and Base-stock

(2) Let the sum of integration values of tokens in all activity circuits for a period be denoted by w. Because of the similar argument in Proposition 6.2, w in the Kanban is equal to that in the Base-stock.

(3) Both Base-stock and Kanban have $\sum_{i=1}^{m} n_i + m + 1$ elementary circuits other than their activity circuits. In the Base-stock, let S_{ij} ($i = 1,2,\ldots,m$ and $j = 1,2,\ldots,n_i$) be the circuit $B_{ij}p_{ij}b_{ij}p_ib_ipbB_{ij}$ with s_{ij} tokens. Also, let S_i ($i = 1,2,\ldots,m$) and S be the circuit $B_ip_ib_ipbB_i$ with s_i tokens, and the circuit $BpbB$ with s tokens, respectively. In the Kanban, let D_{ij} ($i = 1,2,\ldots,m$ and $j = 1,2,\ldots,n_i$) be the circuit $K_{ij}p_{ij}b_{ij}K_{ij}$ with k_{ij} tokens. Also, let D_i ($i = 1,2,\ldots,m$) and D be the circuit $K_ip_ib_iK_i$ with k_i tokens, and the circuit $KpbK$ with k tokens, respectively.

(4) Let the sum of integration values of all connecting queues in the Base-stock and Kanban for a period be W_q^B and W_q^K, respectively. Then,

$$W_q^B \leq \sum_{q \in Q(S_{11})} h_q + \sum_{q \in Q(S_{12})} h_q + \ldots + \sum_{q \in Q(S_{1n_1})} h_q + \sum_{q \in Q(S_{21})} h_q$$
$$+ \sum_{q \in Q(S_{22})} h_q + \ldots + \sum_{q \in Q(S_{2n_2})} h_q + \sum_{q \in Q(S_{m1})} h_q + \sum_{q \in Q(S_{m2})} h_q + \ldots$$
$$+ \sum_{q \in Q(S_{mn_m})} h_q + \sum_{q \in Q(S_1)} h_q + \sum_{q \in Q(S_2)} h_q + \ldots$$
$$+ \sum_{q \in Q(S_m)} h_q + \sum_{q \in Q(S)} h_q + w \qquad (6.10)$$

$$= [s_{11} \cdot L - \rho(h_{11} + h_1 + h)] + [s_{12} \cdot L - \rho(h_{12} + h_1 + h)] + \ldots$$
$$+ [s_{1n_1} \cdot L - \rho(h_{1n_1} + h_1 + h)] + [s_{21} \cdot L - \rho(h_{21} + h_2 + h)]$$
$$+ [s_{22} \cdot L - \rho(h_{22} + h_2 + h)] + \ldots + [s_{2n_2} \cdot L - \rho(h_{2n_2} + h_2 + h)] + \ldots$$
$$+ [s_{m1} \cdot L - \rho(h_{m1} + h_m + h)] + [s_{m2} \cdot L - \rho(h_{m2} + h_m + h)] + \ldots$$
$$+ [s_{mn_m} \cdot L - \rho(h_{mn_m} + h_m + h)] + [s_1 \cdot L - \rho(h_1 + h)] + [s_2 \cdot L - \rho(h_2 + h)]$$
$$+ \ldots + [s_m \cdot L - \rho(h_m + h)] + [s \cdot L - \rho h] + w$$

$$= L \left(\sum_{i=1}^{m} \sum_{j=1}^{n_i} s_{ij} + \sum_{i=1}^{m} s_i + s \right)$$
$$- \rho \left(\sum_{i=1}^{m} \sum_{j=1}^{n_i} h_{ij} + \sum_{i=1}^{m} h_i(n_i + 1) + h \left(\sum_{i=1}^{m} n_i + m + 1 \right) \right) + w. \qquad (6.11)$$

Therefore,

$$W_q^B \leq B \cdot L - \rho \left(\sum_{i=1}^{m} \sum_{j=1}^{n_i} h_{ij} + \sum_{i=1}^{m} h_i(n_i + 1) + h \left(\sum_{i=1}^{m} n_i + m + 1 \right) \right) + w, \qquad (6.12)$$

where,

$$B = \sum_{i=1}^{m}\sum_{j=1}^{n_i} s_{ij} + \sum_{i=1}^{m} s_i + s. \qquad (6.13)$$

As we showed in (6.8),

$$W_q^K = K \cdot L - \rho \left(\sum_{i=1}^{m}\sum_{j=1}^{n_i} h_{ij} + \sum_{i=1}^{m} h_i + h \right) + w.$$

Note that inequality used in (6.10) is because of the existence of some common activities and connecting queues among the elementary circuits in the Base-stock. Now, subtracting W_q^K from both the sides of (6.12), yields

$$W_q^B - W_q^K \leq (B - K)L - \rho \left(\sum_{i=1}^{m} n_i h_i + h \left(\sum_{i=1}^{m} n_i + m \right) \right). \qquad (6.14)$$

If $B - K \leq \dfrac{\sum_{i=1}^{m} n_i h_i + h \left(\sum_{i=1}^{m} n_i + m \right)}{\lambda}$,

then $(B - K)L - \rho \left(\sum_{i=1}^{m} n_i h_i + h \left(\sum_{i=1}^{m} n_i + m \right) \right) \leq 0.$

By (6.14),

$$W_q^B - W_q^K \leq (B - K)L - \rho \left(\sum_{i=1}^{m} n_i h_i + h \left(\sum_{i=1}^{m} n_i + m \right) \right) \leq 0, \text{ or } W_q^B \leq W_q^K.$$

Therefore,

$$W_B = \frac{\rho}{L} \left(\sum_{a \in A} h_a \right) + \frac{1}{L} W_q^B \leq \frac{\rho}{L} \left(\sum_{a \in A} h_a \right) + \frac{1}{L} W_q^K = W_K.$$

Thus, $W_B \leq W_K$. This concludes the proof of part (i).

(5) Now we prove part (ii). If $B = K$, i.e., the total number of cards assigned to the Base-stock be the same as that of the Kanban, then in (6.14),

$$W_q^K - W_q^B \geq \rho \left(\sum_{i=1}^{m} n_i h_i + h \left(\sum_{i=1}^{m} n_i + m \right) \right) > 0, \text{ or } W_q^B < W_q^K. \text{ Thus,}$$

$W_B < W_K$. (Q.E.D.)

In the following, same as Proposition 6.2 and in order to follow the above proof more simply, we rewrite some of the equations given in the proof, but for a more simple assembly production process, where $m = 2$ and $n_1 = n_2 = 2$ (this production process is depicted in Figures 6.3 and 6.5 with the Kanban and Base-stock, respectively). Equation (6. *)' is the simplified form of Equation (6.*).

6.2 Comparison of Kanban and Base-stock

$$W_q^B \leq \sum_{q \in Q(S_{11})} h_q + \sum_{q \in Q(S_{12})} h_q + \sum_{q \in Q(S_{21})} h_q + \sum_{q \in Q(S_{22})} h_q + \sum_{q \in Q(S_1)} h_q$$
$$+ \sum_{q \in Q(S_2)} h_q + \sum_{q \in Q(S)} h_q + w \qquad (6.10')$$

$$= [s_{11} \cdot L - \rho(h_{11} + h_1 + h)] + [s_{12} \cdot L - \rho(h_{12} + h_1 + h)] +$$
$$[s_{21} \cdot L - \rho(h_{21} + h_2 + h)] + [s_{22} \cdot L - \rho(h_{22} + h_2 + h)] +$$
$$[s_1 \cdot L - \rho(h_1 + h)] + [s_2 \cdot L - \rho(h_2 + h)] + [s \cdot L - \rho h] + w$$

$$= (s_{11} + s_{12} + s_{21} + s_{22} + s_1 + s_2 + s)L$$
$$- \rho(h_{11} + h_{12} + h_{21} + h_{22} + 3h_1 + 3h_2 + 7h) + w \qquad (6.11')$$

$$W_q^B \leq B \cdot L - \rho(h_{11} + h_{12} + h_{21} + h_{22} + 3h_1 + 3h_2 + 7h) + w \qquad (6.12')$$

$$B = s_{11} + s_{12} + s_{21} + s_{22} + s_1 + s_2 + s \qquad (6.13')$$

$$W_q^B - W_q^K \leq (B - K)L - \rho(2h_1 + 2h_2 + 6h) \qquad (6.14')$$

Same as the case of the Kanban and CONWIP, the condition in (i) in this proposition does not depend on the processing times in stage 1 (h_{ij}). Also, the right hand side is decided by the structure of the process. Once it is given, the whole performance is decided only by the number of cards, B and K.

6.2.2 Example

By the following example, we show that each converse implications of (i) and (ii) in Proposition 6.3 does not hold.

Example 6.7 This example shows that none of the converse implications in Proposition 6.3 holds true. Consider an assembly production process with $m = 2$ and $n_1 = n_2 = 2$ controlled by Kanban and Base-stock as depicted in Figs. 6.3 and 6.5, respectively. Processing times of $p_{11}, p_{12}, p_{21}, p_{22}, p_1, p_2$ and p are set at 10, 11, 12, 20, 6, 8, and 3 time units, respectively. That is, $h_{11} = 10$, $h_{12} = 11$, $h_{21} = 12$, $h_{22} = 20$, $h_1 = 6$, $h_2 = 8$, and $h = 3$. Same as the previous example, the process p_{22} has two workers, while each of the others has only one worker. Also, initial inventory for every part is set to zero, and it is assumed that sufficient raw materials are always available. Cases 6.7_KAN and 6.7_BAS below show the results for the Kanban and Base-stock, respectively.

Case **6.7_KAN:** Table 6.11 shows the state transition table for a period of the production process with the Kanban. The number of cards are set as $k_{11} = k_{12} = k_{21} = k_1 = k_2 = k = 1$ and $k_{22} = 2$, that is $K = 8$. The system shows a periodic behavior every 12 time units. Activity circuit $p_{21}w_{21}p_{21}$ is critical with maximum cycle mean $\lambda = 12$. Each activity starts once in a period. The throughput is 1/12, and the system WIP is equal to 11.17. That is $W_K = 11.17$.

Table 6.11 State transition of 6.7_KAN for a period

Time	K_{11}	p_{11}	b_{11}	K_{12}	p_{12}	b_{12}	K_1	p_1	b_1	K_{21}	p_{21}	b_{21}	K_{22}	p_{22}	b_{22}	K_2	p_2	b_2	K	p	b	p_d
431	0	1(7)	0	0	1(8)	0	0	1(3)	0	0	1(1)	0	0	----, 1(9)	1	1	----	0	1	----	0	1(12)
432	0	1(6)	0	0	1(7)	0	0	1(2)	0	0	1(12)	0	0	1(20), 1(8)	0	0	1(8)	0	1	----	0	1(11)
434	0	1(4)	0	0	1(5)	0	0	----	1	0	1(10)	0	0	1(18), 1(6)	0	0	1(6)	0	1	----	0	1(9)
438	0	----	1	0	1(1)	0	0	----	1	0	1(6)	0	0	1(14), 1(2)	0	0	1(2)	0	1	----	0	1(5)
439	0	----	1	0	----	1	0	----	1	0	1(5)	0	0	1(13), 1(1)	0	0	1(1)	0	1	----	0	1(4)
440	0	1(10)	0	0	1(11)	0	0	1(6)	0	0	1(4)	0	0	1(12), ----	1	1	----	0	0	1(3)	0	1(3)
443	0	1(7)	0	0	1(8)	0	0	1(3)	0	0	1(1)	0	0	1(9), ----	1	1	----	0	1	----	0	1(12)

Case **6.7_BAS:** The state transition table for a period for the same production process with the Base-stock is given in Table 6.12. The number of cards are set as $s_{11} = s_{12} = s_{21} = 2$, $s_{22} = 3$, and $s_1 = s_2 = s = 1$ (i.e., $B = 12$), which are the minimum number of cards to attain the maximum possible throughput. The system shows a periodic behavior every 12 time units. Circuit $p_{21}w_{21}p_{21}$ is critical with $\lambda = 12$. Each activity starts once in a period. The throughput is 1/12, and the system WIP is equal to 10.83 ($W_B = 10.83$).

Case 6.7_KAN and 6.7_BAS show that neither converse implication of (i) nor (ii) in Proposition 6.3 holds true. Because $W_B = 10.83 < 11.17 = W_K$, but $B \neq K$. Also, $B - K = 12 - 8 > \frac{2h_1 + 2h_2 + 6h}{\lambda} = \frac{2(6) + 2(8) + 6(3)}{12}$.

6.3 Discussion

For an assembly production process analyzed in the Proposition 6.2, some Kanban and CONWIP cases, such as 6.5_KAN and 6.5_CON in Example 6.5, which have the same level of throughput satisfy the if-condition of (i), and then $W_C \leq W_K$ holds. However, in the following, we give an example that dissatisfies the if-condition, and then $W_C > W_K$.[5] In a similar way, in Proposition 6.3 (for the Kanban and Base-stock cases), this example shows that $W_B > W_K$, and of course $B - K > \frac{1}{\lambda} \left(\sum_{i=1}^{m} n_i h_i + h \left(\sum_{i=1}^{m} n_i + m \right) \right)$. This implies that neither CONWIP nor Base-stock is always superior to Kanban.

Example 6.8 Concerning Propositions 6.2 and 6.3, this example shows that both CONWIP and Base-stock do not necessarily outperform Kanban. Consider the production process shown in Figs. 6.2, 6.3, and 6.5 with CONWIP, Kanban, and Base-stock, respectively. The processing times are those in Example 6.5, but we only change the processing time at p from 2 time units to 7. That is, $h_{11} = 10$, $h_{12} = 11$, $h_{21} = 12$, $h_{22} = 20$, $h_1 = 10$, $h_2 = 10$, and $h = 7$. Same as the previous examples, the process p_{22} has two workers, while each of the others has only one worker. Also, initial inventory for every part is set to zero. Cases 6.8_KAN, 6.8_BAS, and 6.8_CON below show the results for Kanban, Base-stock, and CONWIP, respectively.

Case **6.8_KAN:** The state transition table for the production process with the Kanban is given in Table 6.13. Initial cards are set as $k_{11} = k_{12} = k_{21} = k_1 = k_2 = k = 1$ and $k_{22} = 2$, namely $K = 8$. $\lambda = 12$, the throughput is 1/12, and $W_K = 10.33$.

---

[5] we only change the processing time at p in Example 6.5 from 2 to 7 time units

Table 6.12 State transition of 6.7_BAS for a period

Time	B_{11}	p_{11}	b_{11}	B_{12}	p_{12}	b_{12}	B_1	p_1	b_1	B_{21}	p_{21}	b_{21}	B_{22}	p_{22}	b_{22}	B_2	p_2	b_2	B	p	b	p_d
449	0	1(10)	0	0	1(11)	0	0	1(6)	0	1	1(1)	0	0	1(8), 1(20)	1	1	----	0	1	----	0	1(12)
450	0	1(9)	0	0	1(10)	0	0	1(5)	0	0	1(12)	0	0	1(7), 1(19)	0	0	1(8)	0	1	----	0	1(11)
455	0	1(4)	0	0	1(5)	0	0	----	1	0	1(7)	0	0	1(2), 1(14)	0	0	1(3)	0	1	----	0	1(6)
457	0	1(2)	0	0	1(3)	0	0	----	1	0	1(5)	0	0	----, 1(12)	1	0	1(1)	0	1	----	0	1(4)
458	0	1(1)	0	0	1(2)	0	0	----	0	0	1(4)	0	0	----, 1(11)	1	0	----	0	0	1(3)	0	1(3)
459	0	----	1	0	1(1)	0	0	----	0	0	1(3)	0	0	----, 1(10)	1	0	----	0	0	1(2)	0	1(2)
460	0	----	1	0	----	1	0	----	0	0	1(2)	0	0	----, 1(9)	1	0	----	0	0	1(1)	0	1(1)
461	0	1(10)	0	0	1(11)	0	0	1(6)	0	1	1(1)	0	0	1(20), 1(8)	1	1	----	0	1	----	0	1(12)

Table 6.13 State transition of 6.8_KAN for a period

Time	K_{11}	p_{11}	b_{11}	K_{12}	p_{12}	b_{12}	K_1	p_1	b_1	K_{21}	p_{21}	b_{21}	K_{22}	p_{22}	b_{22}	K_2	p_2	b_2	K	p	b	p_d
956	0	1(8)	0	0	1(9)	0	0	1(8)	0	0	1(12)	0	0	1(20), 1(8)	0	0	1(10)	0	0	1(5)	0	1(5)
961	0	1(3)	0	0	1(4)	0	0	1(3)	0	0	1(7)	0	0	1(15), 1(3)	0	0	1(5)	0	1	----	0	1(12)
964	0	----	1	0	1(1)	0	0	----	1	0	1(4)	0	0	1(12), ----	1	0	1(2)	0	1	----	0	1(9)
965	0	----	1	0	----	1	0	----	1	0	1(3)	0	0	1(11), ----	1	0	1(1)	0	1	----	0	1(8)
966	0	1(10)	0	0	1(11)	0	0	1(10)	0	0	1(2)	0	0	1(10), ----	1	1	----	0	0	1(7)	0	1(7)
968	0	1(8)	0	0	1(9)	0	0	1(8)	0	0	1(12)	0	0	1(8), 1(20)	0	0	1(10)	0	0	1(5)	0	1(5)

Case **6.8_BAS:** The state transition table for the Base-stock is given in Table 6.14. Initial cards are set as $s_{11} = s_{12} = s_{21} = 3, s_{22} = 4, s_1 = s_2 = 2, s = 1$, i.e., $B = 18$, which is the minimum number of cards to attain the maximum possible throughput. $\lambda = 12$, the throughput is 1/12, and $W_B = 12.33$.

Case **6.8_CON**: The state transition table is given in Table 6.15. Initial cards are set as $c_{11} = c_{12} = c_{21} = 3$ and $c_{22} = 4$, which are the minimum number of cards to attain the maximum possible throughput. $\lambda = 12$, the throughput is 1/12, and $W_C = 11.25$.

Comparison of the system WIPs in cases 6.8_KAN and 6.8_CON reveals the fact that CONWIP does not necessarily outperform Kanban. Because, $W_K = 10.33 < 11.25 = W_C$. It can be easily verified that the if-condition does not hold, because $N - K = 13 - 8 > \frac{h_1 + h_2 + 3h}{\lambda} = \frac{10 + 10 + 3(7)}{12}$.

This example also shows that Base-stock does not necessarily outperform Kanban, either. Because in cases 6.8_KAN and 6.8_BAS, one can see that $W_K < W_B$ (and of course, $B - K = 18 - 8 > \frac{2h_1 + 2h_2 + 6h}{\lambda} = \frac{2(10) + 2(10) + 6(7)}{12}$).

Therefore, the if-conditions of Propositions 6.2 and 6.3 are meaningful, and as a consequence, both CONWIP and Base-stock are not always superior to Kanban. In fact, a configuration of parameters, such as processing time of activities, number of workers, and number of cards employed in the whole process, decides the superior system in certain situation.

6.4 Conclusions

In this chapter, by using the theory of token transaction system, we compared the performance of the three pull production control systems, Kanban, CONWIP, and Base-stock in assembly production processes.

Concerning the comparison of Kanban with CONWIP and Base-stock, the results showed that Kanban is superior to CONWIP in some cases, while it is not in other cases. Superiority here refers to the fact that the minimum system WIP is smaller than the other to attain the same rate of throughput. This happens in the comparison with Base-stock too. That is, Kanban outperforms Base-stock in some cases, while it does not in other cases. We clarified that the superiority of one over another is determined by a configuration of parameters, such as processing time of activities (except the processing times in stage 1, h_{ij}), number of workers, and number of cards employed in the system as shown in Propositions 6.2 and 6.3. In a certain production system with a configuration, for example, Kanban is superior to CONWIP. Therefore, if a system with such a certain configuration is considered, then it could result in the superiority of Kanban to CONWIP.

Table 6.14 State transition of 6.8_BAS for a period

Time	B_{11}	p_{11}	b_{11}	B_{12}	p_{12}	b_{12}	B_1	p_1	b_1	B_{21}	p_{21}	b_{21}	B_{22}	p_{22}	b_{22}	B_2	p_2	b_2	B	p	b	p_d
954	0	1(10)	0	0	1(11)	0	0	1(10)	1	1	1(7)	0	0	1(8), 1(20)	1	1	1(5)	0	1	----	0	1(12)
959	0	1(5)	0	0	1(6)	0	0	1(5)	0	1	1(2)	0	0	1(3), 1(15)	1	1	----	0	0	1(7)	0	1(7)
961	0	1(3)	0	0	1(4)	0	0	1(3)	0	0	1(12)	0	0	1(1), 1(13)	0	0	1(10)	0	0	1(5)	0	1(5)
962	0	1(2)	0	0	1(3)	0	0	1(2)	0	0	1(11)	0	0	----, 1(12)	1	0	1(9)	0	0	1(4)	0	1(4)
964	0	----	1	0	1(1)	0	0	----	1	0	1(9)	0	0	----, 1(10)	1	0	1(7)	0	0	1(2)	0	1(2)
965	0	----	1	0	----	1	0	----	1	0	1(8)	0	0	----, 1(9)	1	0	1(6)	0	0	1(1)	0	1(1)
966	0	1(10)	0	0	1(11)	0	0	1(10)	1	1	1(7)	0	0	1(20), 1(8)	1	1	1(5)	0	1	----	0	1(12)

Table 6.15 State transition of 6.8_CON for a period

Time	C_{11}	p_{11}	b_{11}	C_{12}	p_{12}	b_{12}	p_1	b_1	C_{21}	p_{21}	b_{21}	C_{22}	p_{22}	b_{22}	p_2	b_2	p	b	p_d
966	0	1(10)	0	0	1(11)	0	1(9)	1	1	1(7)	0	0	1(20), 1(8)	1	1(5)	0	----	0	1(12)
971	0	1(5)	0	0	1(6)	0	1(4)	0	1	1(2)	0	0	1(15), 1(3)	1	----	0	1(7)	0	1(7)
973	0	1(3)	0	0	1(4)	0	1(2)	0	0	1(12)	0	0	1(13), 1(1)	0	1(10)	0	1(5)	0	1(5)
974	0	1(2)	0	0	1(3)	0	1(1)	0	0	1(11)	0	0	1(12), ----	1	1(9)	0	1(4)	0	1(4)
975	0	1(1)	0	0	1(2)	0	----	1	0	1(10)	0	0	1(11), ----	1	1(8)	0	1(3)	0	1(3)
976	0	----	1	0	1(1)	0	----	1	0	1(9)	0	0	1(10), ----	1	1(7)	0	1(2)	0	1(2)
977	0	----	0	0	----	0	1(10)	1	0	1(8)	0	0	1(9), ----	1	1(6)	0	1(1)	0	1(1)
978	0	1(10)	0	0	1(11)	0	1(9)	1	1	1(7)	0	0	1(8), 1(20)	1	1(5)	0	----	0	1(12)

Table 6.16 Parameters in Examples 6.6, 6.7, and 6.8

	Number of workers/ machines	Processing times	Kanban Number of cards	Critical circuit	λ	W_K	CONWIP Number of cards	Critical circuit	λ	W_C	Base-stock Number of cards	Critical circuit	λ	W_B
Example 6.6	$w_{11}=1$ $w_{12}=1$ $w_{21}=1$ $w_{22}=2$ $w_1=1$ $w_2=1$ $w=1$	$h_{11}=10$ $h_{12}=11$ $h_{21}=12$ $h_{22}=20$ $h_1=4$ $h_2=4$ $h=1$	$k_{11}=1$ $k_{12}=1$ $k_{21}=1$ $k_{22}=2$ $k_1=1$ $k_2=1$ $k=1$	$p_{21}w_{21}p_{21}$	12	11.83	$c_{11}=2$ $c_{12}=2$ $c_{21}=2$ $c_{22}=3$	$p_{21}w_{21}p_{21}$	12	11.25				
Example 6.7	$w_{11}=1$ $w_{12}=1$ $w_{21}=1$ $w_{22}=2$ $w_1=1$ $w_2=1$ $w=1$	$h_{11}=10$ $h_{12}=11$ $h_{21}=12$ $h_{22}=20$ $h_1=6$ $h_2=8$ $h=3$	$k_{11}=1$ $k_{12}=1$ $k_{21}=1$ $k_{22}=2$ $k_1=1$ $k_2=1$ $k=1$	$p_{21}w_{21}p_{21}$	12	11.17					$s_{11}=2$ $s_{12}=2$ $s_{21}=2$ $s_{22}=3$ $s_1=1$ $s_2=1$ $s=1$	$p_{21}w_{21}p_{21}$	12	10.83
Example 6.8	$w_{11}=1$ $w_{12}=1$ $w_{21}=1$ $w_{22}=2$ $w_1=1$ $w_2=1$ $w=1$	$h_{11}=10$ $h_{12}=11$ $h_{21}=12$ $h_{22}=20$ $h_1=10$ $h_2=10$ $h=7$	$k_{11}=1$ $k_{12}=1$ $k_{21}=1$ $k_{22}=2$ $k_1=1$ $k_2=1$ $k=1$	$p_{21}w_{21}p_{21}$	12	10.33	$c_{11}=3$ $c_{12}=3$ $c_{21}=3$ $c_{22}=4$	$p_{21}w_{21}p_{21}$	12	11.25	$s_{11}=3$ $s_{12}=3$ $s_{21}=3$ $s_{22}=4$ $s_1=2$ $s_2=2$ $s=1$	$p_{21}w_{21}p_{21}$	12	12.33

References

Khojasteh, Y., & Sato, R. (2015). Selection of a pull production control system in multi-stage production processes. *International Journal of Production Research, 53*(14), 4363–4379.

Khojasteh-Ghamari, Y., & Sato, R. (2011). Managing an assembly production process with a proper control policy. *International Journal of Manufacturing Technology and Management, 22*(1), 2–25.

Sato, R., & Kawai, A. (2007) *Organizing a business process that realizes required throughput: the principle and an application to information systems for SCM* (Discussion Paper Series No. 1184). Department of Social Systems and Management, University of Tsukuba.

Sato, R., & Khojasteh-Ghamari, Y. (2012). An integrated framework for card-based production control systems. *Journal of Intelligent Manufacturing, 23*(3), 717–731.

Conclusions and Future Research 7

In this book, three pull production control systems, Kanban, CONWIP, and Base-stock, were analyzed, and the results of performance comparisons were presented in both serial production lines and assembly production processes. This chapter summarizes the comparison results, presents the conclusions drawn from the analyses, and outlines some suggestions for future studies in the field.

7.1 Serial Production Lines

The comparison between Kanban and CONWIP in serial production lines was completely characterized in Proposition 5.1. CONWIP is superior to Kanban if, and only if, the total number of cards in the CONWIP is less than that in the Kanban. Superiority here refers to the fact that the minimum system WIP is smaller than the other to attain the same rate of throughput. This proposition resolves the complicated situation on comparison between Kanban and CONWIP in serial production lines. It implies that in a serial production line only the total number of cards decides the system performance.

In comparison of the Base-stock with the Kanban and CONWIP, the situation is complicated, such that it cannot be completely characterized. Base-stock was superior to Kanban in some cases, while it was not in other cases. This happened in the comparison with CONWIP too. That is, Base-stock was superior to CONWIP in only few cases. Propositions 5.2 and 5.3 clarified that the superiority of one over another is determined by a configuration of parameters, such as processing time of activities (except the first activity), number of workers, and number of cards employed in the system. In a production line with a certain configuration, for example, Base-stock is superior to Kanban. Therefore, if a line with such configuration was considered, then it could result in the superiority of Base-stock to Kanban.

7.2 Assembly Production Processes

On comparing Kanban with CONWIP and Base-stock in assembly production processes, the results showed that Kanban outperformed CONWIP in some cases, while it did not in other cases. This happened in the comparison with the Base-stock too. That is, Kanban was superior to Base-stock in only some cases. Same as the case of serial production lines, we clarified that the superiority of one over another is determined by a configuration of parameters, such as processing time of activities (but except the processing times in stage 1), number of workers, and number of cards employed in the system as shown in Propositions 6.2 and 6.3. Suppose Kanban is superior to CONWIP in a production system with a certain configuration. Then, if a system with such configuration is considered, then it can result in the superiority of Kanban to CONWIP. As a consequence, there is no general superiority among them as shown in Chap. 6.

7.2.1 Complexity of the Comparisons

Comparison of production control systems can be complicated. A reason is due to the existing of a complex relation among WIP deployment, critical circuits, and throughput. Such examples are Assembly-CONWIP-1 and Assembly-CONWIP-2 cases.[1] Even if we change the number of tokens, the resultant WIP can be still optimum in the sense that the WIP is minimum to attain the changed throughput.

7.3 Limitations and Future Study Directions

1. We assumed that there is an unlimited demand at the output buffer of the last station, and the results discussed in this book are based on this assumption. It has to be seen if they also hold for limited demand. The important performance parameter will then be the ratio between immediately satisfied demand and total demand (service level).
2. We assumed that the system makes a single part type. But, more complex production systems (for example, multi-product manufacturing) can be considered. The analysis would be more complex if different part types and limited demand were considered. In a Kanban, cards (and containers) for each part type are held at each station. In a CONWIP, the cards are not assigned to a defined part type; they rather represent a certain amount of work. It has to be examined how much WIP is held in the Kanban line in comparison to the CONWIP line if more than one part type is considered.
3. We only analyzed the three basic pull production control systems and provided performance comparison among them. The other control systems, such as hybrid

---

[1] See Chap. 6.

Kanban-CONWIP, the extended Kanban, the generalized Kanban can be analyzed and compared with the basic control systems.
4. In simulation experiments of control systems, we found the *optimal* card distributions in each case by a systematic manner. Optimality here refers to a distribution of kanbans by which the maximum throughput for the system with the minimum value of the system WIP is achieved. A procedure can be developed to find the optimal card distributions in those control systems. Such a procedure in the Kanban and Base-stock is more helpful than in the CONWIP especially in assembly production processes, since each of the Kanban and Base-stock depends on two parameters in the system, and many combinations of those parameters. To this, some popular metaheuristics such as genetic algorithms can be considered.

Appendix

List of References

Akturk, M. S., & Erhun, F. (1999). An overview of design and operational issues of Kanban systems. *International Journal of Production Research, 37*, 3859–3881.

Baccelli, F. L., Cohen, G., Olsder, G. J., & Quadrat, J. P. (1992). *Synchronization and linearity – An algebra for discrete event systems*. New York: Wiley.

Berkley, B. J. (1992). A review of the kanban production control research literature. *Production and Operations Management, 1*(4), 393–411.

Bollon, J.-M., Di Mascolo, M., & Frein, Y. (2004). Unified framework for describing comparing the dynamics of pull control policies. *Annals of Operations Research, 125*, 21–45.

Bonvik, A. M., & Gershwin, S. B. (1996). Beyond Kanban: Creating and analyzing lean shop floor control policies (pp. 46–51). In *Manufacturing and service operations management conference proceeding*, Durtmouth College, The Amos Tuck School, Hannover, New Hampshire.

Bonvik, A. M., Couch, C. E., & Gershwin, S. B. (1997). A comparison of production-line control mechanisms. *International Journal of Production Research, 35*(3), 789–804.

Buzacott, J. A. (1989). Queuing models of kanban and MRP controlled production systems. *Engineering Cost and Production Economics, 17*, 3–20.

Dallery, Y., & Liberopoulos, G. (2000). Extended kanban control system: Combining kanban and base stock. *IIE Transactions, 32*, 369–386.

Di Mascolo, M., & Bollon, J.-M. (2011). Use of path algebra tools for a unified description of a large class of pull control policies. *International Journal of Production Research, 49*(3), 611–636.

Duenyas, I. (1994). Estimating the throughput of acyclic assembly system. *International Journal of Production Research, 32*, 1403–1419.

Duenyas, I., & Hopp, W. J. (1992). CONWIP assembly with deterministic processing and random outages. *IIE Transactions, 24*, 97–109.

Duenyas, I., & Hopp, W. J. (1993). Estimating the throughput of an exponential CONWIP assembly system. *Queuing Systems, 14*, 135–157.

Duenyas, I., & Patana-anake, P. (1998). Base-stock control for single product tandem make-to-stock systems. *IIE Transactions, 30*, 31–39.

Duri, C., Frein, Y., & Di Mascolo, M. (2000a). Comparison among three pull control policies: Kanban, base stock, and generalized Kanban. *Annals of Operations Research, 93*, 41–69.

Duri, C., Frein, Y., & Lee, H. S. (2000b). Performance evaluation and design of a CONWIP system with inspections. *International Journal of Production Economics, 64*, 219–229.

Edwards, J. N. (1983). MRP and Kanban – American Style. *APICS 26th Conference Proceedings*, 586–603.

Framinan, J. M., Gonzalez, P. L., & Ruiz-Usano, R. (2003). The CONWIP production control system: Review and research issues. *Production Planning and Control, 14*, 255–265.

Framinan, J. M., Ruiz-Usano, R., & Leisten, R. (2000). Input control and dispatching rules in a dynamic CONWIP flow-shop. *International Journal of Production Research, 38*, 4589–4598.

Gaury, E. G. A., Pierreval, H., & Kleijnen, J. P. C. (2000). An evolutionary approach to select a pull system among Kanban, Conwip and Hybrid. *Journal of Intelligent Manufacturing, 11*, 157–167.

Geraghty, J., & Heavey, C. (2006). A review and comparison of hybrid and pull-type production control strategies. In G. Liberopoulos, C. T. Papadopoulos, B. Tan, J. MacGregor Smith & S. B. Gershwin (Eds.), *Stochastic modeling of manufacturing systems*. Berlin/Heidelberg: Springer.

Gonzlez-R, P.L., Framinan, J.M., & Pierreval, H. (2012). Token-based pull production control systems: An introductory overview. *Journal of Intelligent Manufacturing, 23*(1), 5–22.

Gstettner, S., & Kuhn, H. (1996). Analysis of production control systems kanban and CONWIP. *International Journal of Production Research, 34*(11), 3253–3274.

Hazra, J., & Seidmann, A. (1996) Performance evaluation of closed tree-structured assembly systems. *IIE Transactions, 28*, 591–599.

Hopp, W. J., & Roof, M. L. (1998). Setting WIP levels with statistical throughput control (STC) in CONWIP production lines. *International Journal of Production Research, 36*, 867–882.

Hopp, W. J., & Spearman, M. L. (1991). Throughput of a constant work in process manufacturing line subject to failures. *International Journal of Production Research, 29*, 635–655.

Hopp, W. J., & Spearman, M. L. (2004). To pull or not to pull: What is the question? *Manufacturing & Service Operations Management, 6*(2), 133–148.

Hopp, W. J., & Spearman, M. L. (2008). *Factory physics* (3rd ed.). New York: McGraw-Hill.

Huang, M., Wang, D., & IP, W. H. (1998). Simulation study of CONWIP for a cold rolling plant. *International Journal of Production Economics, 54*, 257–266.

Huang, Y., Kuriger, G., & Chen, F. F. (2013) Simulation studies of hybrid pull systems of kanban and conwip in an assembly line. In A. Azevedo (ed.), *Advances in sustainable and competitive manufacturing systems*. Cham: Springer International Publishing.

Imai, M. (1986). *Kaizen: The key to Japan's competitive success*. New York: McGraw Hill.

Imai, M. (2012). *Gemba Kaizen: A commonsense approach to a continuous improvement strategy* (2nd ed.). New York: McGraw Hill.

Ip, W. H., Huang, M., Yung, K. L., Wang, D., & Wang, X. (2007). CONWIP based control of a lamp assembly production line. *Journal of Intelligent Manufacturing, 18*(2), 261–271.

Khojasteh-Ghamari, Y. (2009). A performance comparison between Kanban and CONWIP controlled assembly systems. *Journal of Intelligent Manufacturing, 20*(6), 751–760.

Khojasteh-Ghamari, Y. (2012). Developing a framework for performance analysis of a production process controlled by Kanban and CONWIP. *Journal of Intelligent Manufacturing, 23*(1), 61–71.

Khojasteh-Ghamari, Y., & Sato, R. (2011). Managing an assembly production process with a proper control policy. *International Journal of Manufacturing Technology and Management, 22*(1), 2–25.

Khojasteh Y., & Sato R. (2015). Selection of a pull production control system in multi-stage production processes. *International Journal of Production Research, 53*(14), 4363–4379

Kimball, G. (1988). General principles of inventory control. *Journal of Manufacturing and Operations Management, 1*(1), 119–130.

Lee, Y.-J., & Zipkin, P. (1992). Tandem queues with planned inventories. *Operations Research, 40*(5), 936–947.

Liberopoulos, G., & Dallery, Y. (2000) A unified framework for pull control mechanisms in multi-stage manufacturing systems. *Annals of Operations Research, 93*, 325–355.

Liker, J. K. (2004). *The Toyota Way: 14 management principles from the world's greatest manufacturer*. New York: McGraw-Hill.

Lödding, H. (2013). Hybrid Kanban/CONWIP control. In H. Lödding (Ed.), *Handbook of manufacturing control*. Berlin/Heidelberg: Springer.

Monden, Y. (2011). *Toyota production system: An integrated approach to just-in-time* (4th ed.). Boca Raton, FL: CRC Press.

Muckstadt, J. A., & Tayur, S. R. (1995). A comparison of alternative kanban control mechanisms: I, background and structural results. *IIE Transactions, 27*(1), 140–150.

Ohno, T. (1988). *Toyota production system: Beyond large scale production*. Cambridge, MA: Productivity Press.

Orlicky, J. (1975). *Material requirements planning: The new way of life in production and inventory management*. New York: McGraw-Hill.

Paternina-Arboleda, C. D., & Das, T. K. (2001). Intelligent dynamic control policies for serial production lines. *IIE Transactions, 33*(1), 65–77.

Pettersen, J. A., & Segerstedt, A. (2009). Restricted work-in-process: A study of differences between Kanban and CONWIP. *International Journal of Production Economics, 118*(1), 199–207.

Renna, P., Magrino, L., & Zaffina, R. (2013). Dynamic card control strategy in pull manufacturing systems. *International Journal of Computer Integrated Manufacturing, 26*(9), 881–894.

Sato, R., & Kawai, A. (2007). *Organizing a business process that realizes required throughput: The principle and an application to information systems for SCM* (Discussion Paper Series No.1184). Department of Social Systems and Management, University of Tsukuba.

Sato, R., & Khojasteh-Ghamari, Y. (2012). An integrated framework for card-based production control systems. *Journal of Intelligent Manufacturing, 23*(3), 717–731.

Sato, R., & Praehofer, H. (1997). A discrete event model of business system – A systems theoretic foundation for information systems analysis: Part 1. *IEEE Transactions on Systems, Man, and Cybernetics, 27*(1), 1–10.

Sharma, S., & Agrawal, N. (2009). Selection of a pull production control policy under different demand situations for a manufacturing system by AHP-algorithm. *Computers and Operations Research, 36*, 1622–1632.

Spearman, M. L., & Zazanis, M. A. (1992) Push and pull production systems: Issues and comparisons. *Operations Research, 40*, 521–532.

Spearman, M. L., Woodruff, D. L., & Hopp, W. J. (1990). CONWIP: A pull alternative to Kanban. *International Journal of Production Research, 23*, 879–894.

Takahashi, K., Myreshka, K., & Hirotani, D. (2005). Comparing CONWIP, synchronized CONWIP, and Kanban in complex supply chains. *International Journal of Production Economics, 93–94*, 25–40.

Wagner, H. M., & Whitin, T. (1958). Dynamic version of the economic lot size model. *Management Science, 5*, 89–96.

Yang, K. K. (2000). Managing a flow line with single-Kanban, dual-Kanban or CONWIP. *Production and Operations Management, 9*(4), 349–366.

Yildiz, G., & Tunali, S. (2008) Response surface methodology based simulation optimization of a CONWIP controlled dual resource constrained system. *International Journal of Advanced Manufacturing Technology, 36*, 1051–1060.

Zhang, W., & Chen, M. (2001). A mathematical programming model for production planning using CONWIP. *International Journal of Production Research, 39*(12), 2723–2734.